PRA
BUBBLES, BOOMS, AND BUSTS

"As one of the top reporters in real estate, Blanche Evans has been a voice of reason for many years and her new book does not disappoint. Blanche takes us through the Great Real Estate Boom of the 21st century, making sense out of the ups and downs and highs and lows of today's dynamic real estate markets. This is a must read for anyone who wants to better understand the past, present, and future of real estate."

David Lereah
Chief Economist
National Association of REALTORS®

"Blanche Evans has proven herself to be an astute observer of the residential real estate industry. In Bubbles, Booms, and Busts, *she takes the reader through the broad range of dynamics impacting the housing market and offers a detailed perspective on the forces driving home ownership in the United States today."*

Richard A. Smith
Vice Chairman and President
Realogy Corporation

"Just in time—Bubbles, Booms, and Busts *further deflates the hype around the 'new' real estate market and helps to demystify one of the most emotional and significant experiences many of us share. Buying or selling a home just got a whole lot easier."*

Tom Reddin
Chief Executive Officer
Lending Tree

Bubbles, Booms, and Busts

Make Money in ANY Real Estate Market

Blanche Evans
Editor of *Realty Times*

McGraw-Hill

New York   Chicago   San Francisco
Lisbon   London   Madrid   Mexico City
Milan   New Delhi   San Juan   Seoul
Singapore   Sydney   Toronto

1 2 3 4 5 6 7 8 9 0   DOC/DOC   0 9 8 7 6

ISBN 13: 978-0-07-147548-8
ISBN 10: 0-07-147548-6

This publication is designed to provide accurate and authoritative information in regard to the subject matter covered. It is sold with the understanding that neither the author nor the publisher is engaged in rendering legal, accounting, futures/securities trading, or other professional service. If legal advice or other expert assistance is required, the services of a competent professional person should be sought.

> —*From a Declaration of Principles jointly adopted by a Committee of the American Bar Association and a Committee of Publishers*

McGraw-Hill books are available at special quantity discounts to use as premiums and sales promotions, or for use in corporate training programs. For more information, please write to the Director of Special Sales, McGraw-Hill Professional, Two Penn Plaza, New York, NY 10121-2298. Or contact your local bookstore.

This book is printed on acid-free paper.

Library of Congress Cataloging-in-Publication Data

Evans, Blanche.
    Bubbles, booms, and busts : make money in any real estate market / by
    Blanche Evans.
       p.   cm.
    Includes index.
    ISBN 0-07-147548-6 (pbk. : alk. paper)
    1. Real estate investment—United States.   2. Residential real estate—United
    States.   3. House buying—United States.   4. House selling—United States.
    I. Title.
HD259.E925   2006
332.63'243—dc22

                                           2006015649

This book is dedicated to my supportive family.
Many thanks to my daughter Lauren, son Sean,
twin-sister Elizabeth Newbury, and
brother Lane Newbury.

CONTENTS

CHAPTER 5

The BUST to Come 107

CHAPTER 6

After the BOOM, BUBBLE, and BUST 131

CHAPTER 7

Make the Current Market Conditions Work for You 155

FOREWORD

The recent real estate boom has made money for an incredible number of households in America. Collectively, property owners' wealth grew by over $4 trillion during this boom period. Home sales registered record numbers for four consecutive years. Housing inventories were lean, and price appreciation was running at high levels. You could say that everything was coming our way during the boom.

I remember what my father told me when he taught me how to drive a car. He said, "When everything is coming your way, you are probably in the wrong lane." I think we can apply that lesson to real estate today. Everything has limits, even real estate markets. They cannot sustain a record-setting sales pace forever. Double-digit price appreciation may be a boon for sellers, but eventually the markets become unaffordable for buyers.

Ever since the boom began in late 2001, some media and Wall Street analysts have been telling us that the roof would cave in for the housing sector. Chicken Little was wrong; the sky did not fall. The housing markets that were fortunate enough to experience the boom have cooled, but have not busted.

Blanche Evans was a steadying and sensible voice during the tumultuous times of the boom and postboom period. She never wavered. She always looked at the fundamentals of the marketplace. She wrote that the Great Real Estate Boom of the twenty-first century was primarily generated by solid fundamentals. It wasn't just low mortgage rates. It was very favorable demographic trends that gave strength to a robust demand for home buying. Over 76 million Baby Boomers were in their peak earning years at the beginning of this decade, and they were buying homes at a record pace. The retiree population was living longer, supporting housing demand. The record immigration of the 1980s and 1990s paid off in the 2000s with immigrant households buying homes for the first time. With the Baby Boomer children entering their first-time home-buying years, I expect strong demand to continue throughout the decade. Moreover, since the 9/11 tragedy, households and investors have viewed property as a safe haven for funds. This has elevated property as a preferred asset among investors and retirees.

I commend Blanche for writing *Bubbles, Booms, and Busts*. She attempts to help you understand the workings of the real estate markets so that you can make informed decisions about your own situation. This book describes the cycles behind bubbles, booms, and busts and examines whether we are in a housing bubble. In the pages that follow, Blanche will be your guide in the world of purchasing real estate.

David Lereah
Chief Economist
National Association of REALTORS®

ACKNOWLEDGMENTS

The top economic and editorial real estate talent of the country helped me with this book. Their personal support, the incredible research their teams performed at my request, and the time and effort they put into making certain that our readers have accurate, up-to-date information has made this book complete.

I can't thank them all enough, but special thanks go to my personal support team:

Jody Lane, publisher of *Realty Times*, for providing me the freedom to work on this book

Carla Davis, copy editor of *Realty Times*, not only for researching and filing for me, but for her insightful suggestions and listening abilities

Larry Jellen, my agent, for taking royal care of me

Dianne Wheeler, my editor at McGraw-Hill, for her expert shepherding of this time-sensitive, yet timeless project

Hugh Siler, my friend and publicist, for his star-making efforts on my behalf

Jeremy Conaway and **John Ansbach**, Recon Intelligence Services, for their encouragement and contributions

For their insights, contributions, and friendship, I am grateful to *Realty Times'* contributors Broderick Perkins, David Reed, Peter Miller, M. Anthony Carr, Ken Harney, Al Heavens, Benny Kass, Jim Crawford, and many others.

I extend very special thanks to the research team of the National Association of REALTORS®. Chief economist David Lereah and senior economist Lawrence Yun of the National Association of REALTORS® did an incredible job of compiling the data for the charts used in this book. Many of these market snapshots were updated specifically to meet our strenuous publication deadline, and for that I am very grateful to these two brilliant economists and their support staff, who all worked very hard.

Additional thanks to:

Leslie Appleton-Young, chief economist, California Association of REALTORS®

Robert Campbell, real estate market timer, www.sandiegorealestate.com

Steve Cook, National Association of REALTORS®, www.Realtor.org

Tom DiMercurio, www.BuyBankHomes.com

Dr. Mark G. Dotzour, chief economist, Real Estate Center at Texas A&M University

Doug Duncan, chief economist, Mortgage Bankers Association

Paul B. Farrell, columnist, CBS Marketwatch

Lee Howlet, president & COO, Fiserv Lending Solutions, www.fiservlendingsolutions.com

Diane Kennedy, CPA, tax, and real estate strategist, www.taxloopholes.com

Dr. Irwin Kellner, economist and columnist CBS, Marketwatch

Frank Nothaft, chief economist, Freddie Mac

Alex Perriello, president and CEO, Realogy Franchise Group

Thomas Prendergast, managed funds professional

Dr. Nicolas Retsinas, Harvard's Joint Center for Housing Studies, www.jchs.harvard.edu

Ralph Roberts, broker, mortgage fraud activist, www.ralphroberts.com

Dan Schmitz, managing director of business specialties, Education, www.REBAC.net

David Seiders, National Association of Home Builders, www.nahb.org

For anyone who assisted me and did not get a mention, please accept my heartfelt apology and private thanks.

Blanche Evans

INTRODUCTION

No matter where you live, whether you own, rent, or live with your parents, you have a vested interest in the housing market. Housing, both new and existing (preowned), impacts about 14 percent of the gross domestic product. That includes sales, remodeling, decorating, furnishings, taxes, moving, landscaping, and numerous other goods and services associated with feathering a nest.

Just as mutual funds and online trading made it possible for the average Joe or Jill to try his or her luck at trading stocks, a number of changes in the way homes are bought and sold are turning homeowners into speculators. Availability of low-barrier mortgages, refinancing options, and two-year homestead-flipping tax benefits has attracted a new breed of real estate junkie.

Whereas Americans once lived and retired in their homes (which explains all those mid-century ranch homes with ashes-of-roses wallpaper, rococo millwork, and orange shag carpet on the market), the modern day-trading American moves approximately every 5.2 years, creating new jobs and excitement wherever he or she goes.

But for every opportunity, there is a greater fool who jumps in after all the money's been made by others. It happened in the 2000 stock market, and investors lost trillions. Worse, it was found that—gasp—many CEOs and their cronies were cooking the books to keep stock values high, at least until they could sell their shares or use their golden parachutes. Since then, the disgraced stock market has see-sawed, and real estate has benefited.

Then, the unthinkable happened. The horrors of terrorist attacks on September 11, 2001, taught a lesson: home is where the heart is. Americans began pouring more investment than ever into housing, spurred by generous flushes of cash, courtesy of the Federal Reserve's lowered short-term rates. Easy mortgage products chipped in to help, with a strong secondary market buying back most loans so that lenders were free to lend again.

By 2005, housing had been on a nine-year bull run, breaking annual sales records for five years straight. The national home-ownership rate approached nearly 70 percent, and by 2006 more than one out of four home buyers were buying either a second home or residential property for an investment. National vacancy rental rates were at an all-time high. Savings sank to zero. Consumer debt ratios soared. In addition, still smarting from soap in the eyes caused by ignoring the "Internet bubble," the media has been relentless in making and keeping "the housing bubble" a hot topic.

The nation is fascinated because, as real estate columnist Peter Miller puts it, "Most of us prefer to live indoors." And that is where the roof meets the brick. Unlike other investments that simply make or lose money; we *need* housing.

That is the reasoning behind this book. It is laid out to include everything you need to know to understand housing markets and how they work. You will learn what a bubble is, what causes bubbles, and whether a bubble is forming or bursting in your area. You will learn the fundamentals of home buying as an investment—both long and short term—how to choose, hold, and enhance the value of your property.

Although this book is filled with interesting statistics, charts, and studies that are based on the most recent information, please do not assume that this data has an expiration date. There is no reason this book cannot be the go-to primer for understanding real estate markets for years into the future.

The book is divided into seven chapters:

Chapter 1 explains what housing bubbles, booms, and busts really are and introduces you to the concept of the "rolling boom," where home buyers move to the next "hot" area for jobs and investment. You'll learn what caused the housing boom of 2001 to 2006, including government incentives, easy money, lack of other viable investments, and other reasons.

Chapter 2 introduces first-time home buyers and their impact on the marketplace. Generational differences and preferences, cultural diversity, and profit motivations all lead to *who* is buying homes.

Chapter 3 investigates *where* people are moving and *why* and what those migration patterns mean to city growth and home types and preferences.

Chapter 4 outlines the difference between national "bubbles" and metro markets, with insights into risk evaluation. Previous housing booms and busts are dissected, along with present dangers to the current market such as mortgage fraud and debt addiction.

Chapter 5 explores the bust to come. With the federal government slowing housing by manipulating interest rates, it's a sure bet they won't land that plane on a dime, but don't be fooled into thinking your home is losing value, even if it does so temporarily. Of greater concern should be the government's attempt to do away with homeowner benefits such as the mortgage interest rate deduction. The chapter also includes studies and forecasts about two of the hottest markets—California and Las Vegas.

Chapter 6 will teach you how to wait out a buyer's market, prepare your home to maximize gains, take advantage of tax credits, and other ways you can make money on real estate, particularly if you get out of your own way by not being too greedy. You'll learn what the rental outlook is so you can decide whether or not you want to be a landlord. You will also see that even if the market contracts temporarily, it will still move forward, providing you, as a homeowner, return on your money.

Chapter 7 will show you how to invest in real estate wisely, so that you can survive and thrive in any market by choosing the right home, the right loan, and the right time to buy and sell without being driven by fear.

After finishing this book, you will thoroughly understand how the housing market works and what you can expect when you buy or sell a home—in *any* market.

CHAPTER 1

THE CURRENT HOUSING BUBBLE—CAUSE AND EFFECT

What Is a Housing Bubble?

A bubble is about economics, and it can form in any market where speculative mania can make an attractive market go through the proverbial roof. According to the Center for Economic and Policy Research, home prices have risen more than 45 percent since 1996 (after adjusting for inflation), creating more than $5 trillion in "bubble wealth" or the equivalent of $70,000 per family of four.

Back in 1998, oil was $10 a barrel. Today it is hovering between $70 and $80 a barrel, but you do not hear talk of an "oil bubble." So, why then is the word *bubble* being used so frivolously about buying something as fundamental as a house? There is a long list of reasons why the term is being used, but with very few solid definitions:

> www.reference.com suggests, "an economic bubble occurs when speculation in a commodity causes the price to increase, thus producing more speculation. The price of the good then reaches absurd levels and the bubble is usually followed by a sudden drop in prices, known as a crash."

> Wikipedia calls the housing bubble a type of economic bubble that is characterized by "rapid increases in the valuations of real property such as housing until they reach unsustainable levels relative to incomes and other economic indicators, followed by decreases that can result in many owners holding negative equity" (or mortgage debt higher than the value of the property).

Even financial experts cannot agree on the
definition of a housing bubble.

The Mortgage Banker's Association, in its September 2005 analysis of housing and mortgage markets, suggested that when describing a bubble, analysts and economists mean different things. "[Housing] analysts use the term *bubble* simply to mean an above-average house price appreciation rate," says the report. "However, economists and financial market analysts generally reserve the term *bubble* for speculative behavior: purchasing an asset exclusively with the intent to resell it for a gain, which leads to price movements that are detached from the economic fundamentals of supply and demand."

Even with the variations of definitions, it seems safe to say, a *housing bubble* exists when rapid gains in the valuation of real property reach unsustainable levels relative to fundamentals such as household income. Following this pattern of thought, a bubble popping would be a rapid decrease in equity or value. Yet, several economists say they do not see a bubble in the current nation's housing.

EXPERT'S VIEW

David Lereah, chief economist of the National Association of REALTORS®, said he does not believe a real estate bubble exists. "Just when you think sales activity is ready to settle into a more sustainable pace, the housing market continues to surprise," said Lereah. "Job growth and economic improvement are boosting home sales."

EXPERT'S VIEW

Freddie Mac's chief economist, Frank Nothaft, agreed with Lereah when he said, "We believe that the housing industry, although poised to ease a bit, will still continue to bustle as the economy continues to expand steadily and long-term rates remain affordable."

Although economists do not all agree about which conditions can cause a housing bubble to rise and pop, most agree that jobs, demographics, mortgage interest rates, housing costs, and consumer attitudes are a few factors that would be relevant. However, at what point can a bubble be identified—when prices go up? Or could that be simply inflation? Conversely, when prices moderate, is that deflation, or is a bubble bursting?

If you think of inflation (the upward price movement of goods and services in an economy) as air and speculative fever as the blower, it is easy to see how bubbles can develop: people *believe* they are making good investments. It is also easy to see how bubbles pop: people suddenly believe it's time to get out of an investment. Investors seek to sell what they have "at the top" and get out, or they sit on the sidelines and do not buy in until buying conditions improve. Or they move their money to another suitcase, another town. This produces what Lereah calls a "rolling boom," when speculative fever cools in one area and moves to another where there is more promise to buy low and sell high. An example of this is when the speculative money moves from the California desert to Las Vegas and from Las Vegas to Dallas.

Over the last 30 years, according to the Office of Federal Housing Enterprise Oversight (OFHEO), the HUD subsidiary commissioned to oversee the "capital adequacy and financial safety" of government-sponsored enterprises (GSEs) Fannie Mae and Freddie Mac, house prices have risen approximately 6 percent annually. However, in the first quarter of 2005, they had risen 12.5 percent. (See Figure 1.1.)

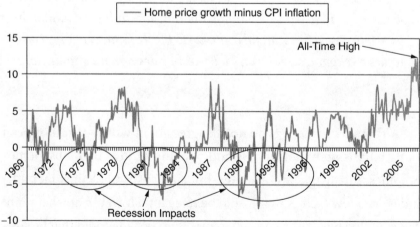

Figure 1.1 *Real Home Price Growth*
Source: National Association of REALTORS®

Gains were spread across the states, but some coastal areas experienced as much as double-digit gains well above 20 percent. Thus, a more reasonable explanation of what's been happening over the past several years is a housing *boom*.

Bubbles and Booms

A lot of factors can stimulate a boom in a given location, such as tax relief, interest rates, retirement plans, jobs, and builder incentives, to name just a few. There is also the gold rush mentality—hearing there is a boom tends to make people behave as if there is one, and more will flock to cash in on the area. Never in recent history have conditions converged in such perfect harmony to favor buying a home—from government subsidies to homeowners to the failure of the stock market to provide fair gains for the average investor, just to name a few.

There is plenty of evidence that some real estate booms have taken place, most recently from 2001 to 2005, when home price appreciation leaped into the double digits and broke existing records for five years straight. "Keep in mind, there has not been a national 'bubble' since data collection began in 1968," says Walt Molony, senior associate of the National Association of REALTORS® (NAR). However, data points change over the years, as they become more or less significant. For example, comparisons for median prices are with the same period a year earlier because of a seasonality in family buying patterns. Older existing-home sales data, 1968 through 1988, is based on an earlier benchmark, as are condo sales for 1981 through 1988. In addition, the condo market has undergone a maturation process, with new tax laws allowing empty-nesters to trade down from a large

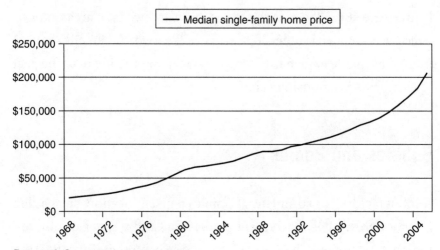

FIGURE 1.2   *National Home Price*
Source: National Association of REALTORS®

single-family home to a well-appointed yet lower-cost condo without a tax hit. (See Figure 1.2.)

As Figure 1.1 shows, price declines do happen, but rarely. These declines usually require two conditions to take place: oversupply of homes for sale in a local market and adverse economic impact—mainly job losses. Although one can always find exceptions to any data, it is useful to note that price declines (when they occurred) were relatively short lived (several years) in most metro areas. Most people who go through such corrections, but stay in their homes for a normal period of home ownership, still net healthy gains. Some metros, especially those in the Midwest and South, have never experienced price declines, which is one of the major reasons the United States has not experienced an overall price decline. (This data is based on records kept since 1968 by the National Association of REALTORS®.)

Since 1968, the median home price has risen (Figure 1.2), on average, at a percentage point or two above the rate of inflation, otherwise known as the consumer price index (CPI). (Obviously we have been above that number for the last five years with historically tight inventory, which is just now improving.) The historic average—6.4 percent—appears high due to a period of high (double-digit) inflation in the late 1970s and early 1980s.

ROLLING BOOMS

As opportunity and affordability diminish, homebuyers, particularly young buyers, pull up stakes and move to other areas, sometimes creating boomtowns along the way. In his book *Are You Missing the Real Estate Boom?*, National Association of REALTORS® chief economist David Lereah writes that a first-time buyer in Anaheim, California, who purchased a $300,000 home at the end of 2001 experienced a 16.1 percent price appreciation in 2002 and an 18 percent appreciation in 2003. Another example is that a buyer in the Nassau-Suffolk, Long Island, New York area purchased a $300,000 home and experienced a 26 percent appreciation in 2002 and only a 16.5 percent appreciation in 2003. The housing boom continues to be stimulated as buyers roll their gains from some areas into new communities that are less expensive, but offer potential for even higher equity gains.

Will gains continue? Likely not, but that does not mean that housing is headed for a bust either.

A five-year bull run in housing, with some markets appreciating at 20 to 30 percent, has to end sooner or later, which is raising fears that housing may pop like a bubble. Bubbles are neither sustainable nor desirable and a return to a more normal market is inevitable. (See Figure 1.3.)

	First quarter 2005	Second quarter 2005
Las Vegas	52%	12%
Reno	16%	32%

Washington, D.C.	31%	26%
Baltimore	9%	17%

San Diego	21%	8%
Phoenix	24%	47%

FIGURE 1.3 *Rolling Boom*
Source: National Association of REALTORS®

EXPERT'S VIEW

*"Simply stated, a real estate boom is a healthy real estate expansion,"
says Lereah. "A pullback in prices for a year or so is nothing to
get upset about. A one-year dip is just a blip in the long-term
expansion path." Why? "Even when property sales and price
appreciation settle back to more normal levels of activity, property returns still offer benefits that more traditional investment
vehicles cannot. The leverage power of real estate investments, as
well as its tax benefits, gives real estate a 'competitive edge' over
stocks, bonds, and other long-term investments—even in a slow
real estate market."*

It is easy to see why houses have become the new stock market.
When a person buys $100,000 worth of stock, he or she pays $100,000
or buys on a relatively unforgiving "margin." That stock is subject to a
number of variables that push it up and down in value, from the whims
of day traders to the integrity of its management to its competition
and to world, national, and local news. That means that once the

stock is purchased, the only control the stockholder has remaining is when to sell.

But a $100,000 home can be financed with OPM (other people's money) up to 100 percent, and even beyond. Even if a home only appreciates a percent or two ahead of inflation, in five years it could be worth 15 percent more than it was at the time of purchase. By the time the homeowner deducts the mortgage interest and property taxes, he or she has lived in the home essentially for free—or, at the least, at a substantial discount over renting and the buildup of equity, or ownership.

And that's before any capital gains on the sale of the home.

Specific Causes of the Current Housing Boom

Despite the anticipated cooling of housing in 2006, whether the nation is in a housing bubble remains to be seen; but it is definitely true that we are in a *housing boom*. After a nine-year run, and five years of record sales, housing was still hot through 2006 and approached previous records set in 2003 and 2004. The average house gained 13.4 percent in resale value between the second quarter of 2004 and the same period in 2005. Despite slower sales through the first half of 2006, home prices continue to rise. Price gains in California, Nevada, Florida, and other areas have been legendary, with double-digit increases year after year. As they are discovered by hungry baby boomers before retirement, areas that have never before experienced housing inflation are now being affected—yet another factor in the "rolling boom."

EXAMPLE

Prescott, Arizona, home prices increased 40 percent in 2005, but it clearly was not all about warm weather retirement. Fargo, North Dakota, which is hardly Sunbelt beachfront, also saw 10 percent increases (and that is nine years after the movie "Fargo" first came out).

High returns are a far cry from the plodding, reliable, inflation-based price gains of the last 50 years (before the housing boom began in the late 1990s). Home prices usually track a point or two ahead of inflation. If inflation is held to about 2 or 3 percent, home prices nose ahead about 4 to 5 percent annually, bringing a nice tidy return in exchange for the maintenance chores of home ownership.

Except for local economic shocks, like the collapse or exit of a major employer, home prices nationwide have not gone down since the Great Depression. Nearly 70 percent of the nation's population owns a home. In 2004 and 2005, more than one-third of home buyers bought either a second home or a home to rent out as an investment. The Federal Reserve tracked lending practices, noting that nearly 9 percent of loans were for investment properties, up nearly 2 percent from the previous year.

That begs the question: What is causing
the present housing boom?

Although each market behaves differently because of local economic and desirability factors, the following factors certainly play a part in every locale:

- Buyers' market versus sellers' market
- The American dream
- Tax benefits
- Low-entry loan products
- Low-interest rates and liquidity
- Underperforming stock market

It stands to reason that any changes in these factors could also precipitate a bust or a "bubble burst." The more risks there are and the more they are layered, the higher the risk of a housing bust.

BUYERS' MARKETS VERSUS SELLERS' MARKETS

A buyers' market exists when there are more homes for sale than buyers, giving buyers the negotiating advantage. This type of market is characterized by long marketing periods (over six months, generally) and lots of concessions by the sellers in terms, price, and financing.

Keep in mind that a market can be defined as small as a cul-de-sac or as large as an MSA (metropolitan statistical area). Most real estate practitioners consider a balanced market to be one where homes take about six months to sell. Sometimes a buyers' market can occur overnight. The exit of one or more major employers from a community, a natural disaster such as a flood or earthquake, or some other catastrophic event can affect home values for years. The homeowners who are most hurt in a buyers' market are those with little or no equity built into the home. If they are forced to sell, they may have to come to the closing table with cash to pay their mortgage off or allow the home to be repossessed by the lender.

In contrast, a sellers' market is when there are more buyers than homes for sale. Prices go up, concessions disappear, and sellers quickly find that selling is a mixed blessing. They make money, but when they buy again, those houses have gone up in price too. This causes them to put down less, accept a larger mortgage, or move to the next "rolling boom" town.

A community can suddenly become "hot," with a lot of word of mouth created by people who have already made money or who are talking about the next boom and making it self-fulfilling. As the housing market becomes more competitive for sellers, buyers realize that their interest is at a premium, and they increase their demands to sellers. Those nice chandeliers that normally would not be included in the purchase price of the home now become a bargaining chip for the buyer. The buyer may ask the seller to provide a home warranty at the seller's expense or request that the seller pay more of the closing costs than usual out of the settlement proceeds.

Although a boom occurs when there is a sustained sellers' market and a bust is the result of a sustained buyers' market, the only certainty is that one side of the market will never stay on top forever. Following are some specific factors that impact the ups and downs in the housing market.

The American Dream

The personal, political, and economic freedom that America offers allows everyone to rise above their circumstances. All it takes is hard work and perseverance toward a goal, says the myth. Usually, that goal is wealth, and with financial success comes the ability to own property.

As immigrants established this democracy, "pulling yourself up by your own bootstraps" became the American way. Settlers found that home ownership was not only surprisingly within reach, but they could buy more home for the money than where they came from.

Home ownership is in the genetic code of today's Americans. Owning versus renting has many pros and cons, but since you have to sleep somewhere, the conventional wisdom is that you are either building equity for yourself or for someone else.

When you are an owner, you can have a pet of any size, paint the walls, house extra friends and relatives, and skinny dip in your pool. These kinds of choices are appealing.

Home ownership, with its attendant responsibilities, historically slow equity buildup, and high transaction costs, is a long-term investment that means you are likely to stay put for a while. This causes you to take more interest in your community—America at the local level. That is why the federal and state governments do everything in their power to make it attractive for almost anyone to buy a home—from opening federal floodgates of money to arresting fraudsters who try to cheat home buyers. It sees home ownership as an opportunity to stabilize communities at both the macro and local levels.

President Bush has said he would like to see home ownership at 75 percent—a rate that would mean the majority of families (and minorities) would become homeowners. The U.S. Department of Housing and Urban Development is mandated to:

1. Promote home ownership, particularly among minorities
2. Create affordable opportunities for low-income home buyers
3. Support the homeless, elderly, and disabled

THE TAXPAYER RELIEF ACT OF 1997

At last count, nearly 69 percent of Americans owned their own homes, and one out of four baby boomers own more than one home, says the NAR. In 2004–2005 more than one-third of home buyers bought either a second home or a house as an investment. (See Figure 1.4.) What is inciting all this home buying? One of the most compelling benefits of

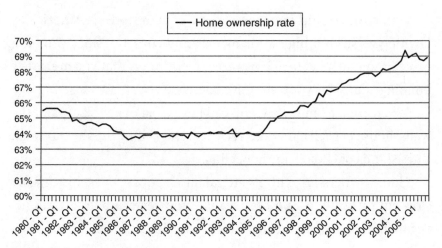

FIGURE 1.4 *Home Ownership Rate*
Source: U.S. Census Bureau

home ownership is tax relief. In fact, you can date the boost in the current housing boom to the passage of the Taxpayer Relief Act of 1997. One of the areas most affected by the law is housing, where huge profits gained by the sale of personal residences are exempted by meeting easy qualifications. A seller must have owned and used the home as his or her principal residence for two of the last five years before the home is sold. Married couples filing jointly can exclude up to $500,000 in capital gains, and singles can exclude up to $250,000—after only two years! Even better, lucky homeowners can do this over and over without having to reinvest their capital gains in housing as they once did.

The Taxpayer Relief Act of 1997 provided the liquidity and the incentives necessary to make it profitable to move. Even though most of what we know about the impact of the Taxpayer Relief Act is anecdotal, we do know that before 1997 homes were not as easy to liquidate *and* only the wealthy could afford second homes. The new law meant that homeowners could pull equity out of their homes and use it to buy other properties.

With the advent of low interest and low down payment loans, home buyers are able to purchase property with little money down and relatively little money invested during the life of the loan. This gives homeowners the ability to get out in two years and pocket a profit—tax-free. It would take an act of Congress to overturn the Taxpayer Relief Act of 1997, so home buyers are taking advantage and enjoying the benefits while they can.

What can go wrong?

What the government "giveth," the government can "taketh" away. Just ask anyone in midlife crisis if they remember the good old 1980s, when credit card and car loan interest payments could be deducted from federal income taxes. And like that distant memory, some in the government, such as the president's Tax Reform Panel in 2005, are hoping that the time will come when consumers will forget they were once also able to deduct their mortgage interest payments.

ACCESSIBLE, LOW-BARRIER LOAN PRODUCTS

It takes liquidity to enable home buyers to move from place to place. Accessible, low-barrier loan products allow homeowners to capitalize on rising appreciation with little investment. Keeping the money flowing are Freddie Mac (Federal Home Loan Mortgage Corporation) and Fannie Mae (Federal National Mortgage Association), which buy the loans from the lenders and sell them to investors in the secondary market, freeing the lenders to lend more money. This has reduced risk for lenders, allowing the creation of new loan products to be introduced to consumers.

Very few home buyers take advantage of the full term of their mortgage notes, which is one reason why the adjustable-rate mortgage has escalated in use. With the average first-time home buyer moving within 5.2 years and second home buyers staying an average of 4 to 11 years, the 30-year fixed-rate mortgage has lost relevance with many of today's consumers, particularly while interest rates drop. Why pay more interest for a term length you'll never need?

In February 2004, then Federal Reserve Chairman Alan Greenspan suggested that "many homeowners might have saved tens of thousands of dollars had they held adjustable-rate mortgages rather than fixed-rate mortgages during the past decade, though this would not have been the case, of course, had interest rates trended sharply upward." Fixed mortgage payments are safer because the terms do not change over the life of the loan. However, the cost of this protection is higher fees to guard the lender from rising interest rates and potential loss of refinancing business.

Greenspan encouraged lenders to create mortgage product alternatives to the traditional fixed-rate mortgage. "To the degree that households are driven by fears of payment shocks but are willing to manage their own interest rate risks, the traditional fixed-rate mortgage may be an expensive method of financing a home," said the Fed chairman.

Adjustable-Rate Mortgages (ARMs)

Adjustable-rate mortgages offer interest rates that are lower than fixed-rate mortgages, but the disadvantage is that they can go up or down at the end of their terms, causing payment shocks to borrowers. Like fixed rates, the popularity of adjustable-rate mortgages depends upon current economic trends and the money market index to which they are tied.

Explains *Realty Times* real estate columnist Broderick Perkins, "To come up with the ARM rate, the lender will add a 'margin,' usually two to four percentage points, to the index. An ARM's lower initial rate typically is lower than the fixed rate from about a quarter point to two points or more. When the first adjustment occurs (typically from

6 months to 1, 3, 5, 7, and 10 years) and how often the rate adjusts depends upon the terms of the loan. After the first adjustment occurs, subsequent adjustments typically occur every six months or once a year. The adjustment period is disclosed in the loan terms."

ARMs also generally have a limit or "cap" on how high they can move during each adjustment period, as well as how high they can move over the life of the loan, in order to protect borrowers from drastic payment fluctuations.

EXPERT'S VIEW

ARMs are irresistible in an appreciating housing market, even if they expose the borrower to more risk. "Comparing the average one-year ARM rate with the average fixed-rate mortgage on a $250,000 loan, you'll spend about $300 less a month on your mortgage payment during the initial one-year rate period," says Broderick Perkins.

Some new loan products include "hybrids" that are a combination of fixed and adjustable rates. Hybrid terms can offer a low, fixed rate for 1, 2, 5, or 10 years before they roll over to an adjustable rate. However, that adjustable rate can be higher or lower than the original fixed term—again exposing the borrower to payment shock.

Interest-Only Loans (IOs)

Newer loans make the adjustable-rate mortgage appear downright tame. Lender Henry Savage explains the appeal of the interest-only loan, where a borrower pays only the interest for a fixed period—3 to 10 years—with no money allocated to pay down the principal (the borrowed amount of the home).

Interest-only loans allow the monthly payment to be equal to only the interest charged for that month. The principal balance does not change. In contrast, a loan that carries a 30-year amortization requires a monthly payment that covers the interest charged, plus enough of the principal balance to pay the loan down to zero in 30 years. An interest-only payment can be lower by as much as 20 percent, regardless of how much you borrow, allowing the buyer to purchase 20 percent more house. As an example, a $400,000 loan with a 30-year amortization at 5.75 percent will cost $2,334 per month. An interest-only payment would only cost $1,917 per month.

EXAMPLE

Henry Savage explains, "Let's say that your comfort level for a house payment is $2,700 per month. Subtract $400 for the real estate taxes and insurance, and you have $2,300 left to make the principal and interest (or just interest) payment. At 5.75 percent, a 30-year amortized loan would allow you to borrow $394,000. An interest-only loan would allow you to borrow $480,000."

Option ARMs

Option ARMs allow the borrower to pay less than the interest due. If a payment is not adequate, the mortgage balance grows accordingly. This is a loan favored by investors, but it is also one of the first to be targeted by tightening lending standards. The use of such a loan can indicate the buyer cannot really afford the full monthly payment and is gambling on appreciation at resale. More than any other loan, an option loan can put the borrower "upside down," so that the additional mortgage due makes it impossible to sell the property without bringing money to the table.

Piggyback Loan

The *piggyback loan* is another high-risk product where a second mortgage is "piggybacked" onto the first mortgage. This kind of loan is used to compensate when a buyer is unable to come up with a large down payment or any payment at all. While this loan helps the buyer to leverage the transaction and avoid paying private mortgage insurance, it can be a red flag indicating that the borrower is not financially ready to buy a home.

Consumers Love Risk

A recent *Wall Street Journal* Online/Harris Interactive Personal Finance Poll found that nearly one in five (19 percent) U.S. adults who purchased a home within the last three years for their primary residence say they spent *above* their suggested price range, while two-thirds (67 percent) stayed within their price range, and 12 percent were below their price range.

Home buyers who used a mortgage broker, direct lender, or another source were nearly three times more likely to obtain a fixed-rate mortgage, but an astounding one-third (34 percent) opted for a creative mortgage such as:

Interest-only mortgage. Where borrowers pay interest but no principal for a fixed period at the beginning of the loan (17 percent)

Piggyback mortgage. Where the loan combines a standard first mortgage with a home-equity loan or line of credit to avoid private mortgage insurance or the higher interest rates on jumbo loans (10 percent)

Payment option mortgage. Where borrowers have four payment options each month, and those who elect to make the minimum payment could actually see their loan balance rise rather than fall (5 percent)

Miss-a-payment mortgage. Where borrowers are allowed to skip up to 2 mortgage payments a year and up to 10 payments over the life of the loan without ruining their credit rating (2 percent)

Regional differences were also obvious. With fewer than 17 percent of home buyers able to buy the median-priced home in California in 2005, it is not surprising to find that home buyers on the West Coast (29 percent) were much more likely to have bought beyond their suggested price range. The more conservative Northeast (8 percent) and Midwest (12 percent) home buyers were less likely to incur such risk. But Southern home buyers, driven by gains in Florida and the Gulf Coasts of Mississippi and Alabama, were slightly less risk-averse (22 percent).

So long as lenders do not require high barriers to lend money, borrowers are likely to continue to buy their homes using other people's money in anticipation of capital gains when they sell.

What can go wrong?

Rising home prices have kept loan defaults relatively low, because most loans are "new" (less than five years old and under 7 percent in interest), but that could change if adjustable-rate and high-risk mortgages become too expensive for borrowers to handle.

Lenders can decide that they need to lower their risk by raising lending standards.

The government is already encouraging Fannie Mae and Freddie Mac to limit their risk by curbing the number of "exotic" loans they buy back to package into securities for the secondary market.

EXPERT'S VIEW

Then Federal Reserve Chairman Alan Greenspan told the nation's bankers in 2005, "The apparent froth in housing markets may have spilled over into mortgage markets. The dramatic increase in the prevalence of interest-only loans as well as the introduction of other, more exotic forms of adjustable-rate mortgages are developments that bear close scrutiny. To be sure, these financing vehicles have their appropriate uses. But to the extent that some households may be employing these instruments to purchase a home that would otherwise be unaffordable—their use is adding to the pressures in the marketplace."

Concern with this possible added pressure in the marketplace has caused Fannie Mae and Freddie Mac to announce at a lending conference that they would not be part of the problem. "We are here to work with lenders to develop markets, not exploit them," Connie Ferran, Freddie Mac's vice president of regional lending for the western states, told a lending conference. "That is why we will not buy loans that we know will end up in foreclosure or were originated with predatory lending practices."

In other words, these government-sponsored enterprises (GSEs) will take a "cautious" approach to what is often referred to as "exotic" loans. The good news for borrowers is that, in general, the government-sponsored lenders agree that higher-risk mortgages make financial sense in some cases, but not for the borrower who is stretching beyond reason to get into an unaffordable home. To that end, both of these agencies are working on new presale requirements and flexible credit standards to continue housing growth.

LOW INTEREST RATES AND LIQUIDITY

If you are pinching yourself with joy that mortgage interest rates are still hovering near or not much above historic lows, enjoy it while it lasts—because it will not go on forever. Buyers all over the nation are taking advantage of continuing record-low interest rates, even while the federal government attempts to influence long-term rates by raising short-term rates.

What goes down—must go up!

Long-term mortgage rates like those on the 30-year fixed-rate mortgage are largely determined by the yield on the 10-year Treasury bond. When the bond yield falls, so do long-term mortgage rates. Risk of inflation due to economic growth, sudden price hikes in key consumables (like oil), and other similar economic factors can cause the bond yield to fall. When short-term rates rise, as when the Federal Reserve raises overnight rates, consumers can expect to pay more interest on debt such as credit cards and home equity loans. However, the bond market is a little more unpredictable. "It is important to understand that the federal government has complete control over certain short-term interest rates, such as the federal funds rate and the discount rate. But long-term interest rates, such as the yield on Treasury bonds or a 30-year, fixed-rate mortgage, are controlled by market forces," explains Henry Savage, columnist for *Realty Times.*

When investors are buying bonds and causing long-term interest rates to drop, that means they are not optimistic about the economy.

When inflation rears its ugly head, mortgage interest rates can go through the roof.

That's one thing that can go wrong.

One reason some believe the nation is in a housing bubble is that interest rates on mortgages have been historically low for so long that it was inevitable that they turn in the other direction. This puts a cramp in the housing market by reducing the number of buyers who qualify for certain loans and the homes they want to buy. Interest rates can go up dramatically, putting more pressure on home buyers economically and psychologically. Every increase impacts the monthly payments a home buyer will have, particularly those with adjustable-rate or hybrid loans.

EXAMPLE

Savage explains, "Let's say a home buyer wants a $165,000 fixed-rate loan at 5.8 percent, with a monthly payment of $968.14, excluding escrows for taxes and insurance. In one day, the rate can go up. At 6.07 percent, the same loan now costs $996.70, adding $28.56 per month, or $10,200 over the life of the loan. (A rise of a single point in interest can cost $100 more per month, adding $40,000 to the life of the loan.)"

When interest rates rise, it is easy to understand why home buyers try to leverage more house with an adjustable-rate mortgage. However, this is a dangerous game to play if you plan to be in the home when the interest rate resets to a more expensive interest payment.

EXAMPLE

Savage explains, "Let's say you are buying a starter home with a loan amount of $65,000. You have a one-year adjustable-rate mortgage (ARM) at (index rate plus margin) 10 percent, but your lender is offering an 8 percent rate for the first year. With the 8 percent rate, your first-year monthly payment would be only $476.95. But when the discount runs out and your loan resets to 10 percent, your next year's payment is $568.82. Suppose that the index rate increases 2 percent in one year and the ARM rate rises to a level of 12 percent? (That is an increase of almost $200 in your monthly payment.)"

In addition, there is the psychological variable. Today's home buyers know only easy credit. They began getting credit cards in high school so that the companies could get them hooked on debt. By the time they start shopping for a home, all they know is that interest rates have

EXPERT'S VIEW

A lot of folks, me included, thought rates this year would be significantly higher given the massive federal deficit, our woeful balance of trade problems, the OPEC tax, and those higher oil prices. With this view, the great financial miracle of our day is not that mortgage rates have again reached over 6 percent, it's that they're not substantially higher," says Peter Miller, author of The Common-Sense Mortgage *(Contemporary Books, 1999).*

always been below 7 percent, since they have been 7 percent since before 1998. That's a long time—long enough to establish a new norm. So what will happen when interest rates rise back to 7 or 8 percent— levels that used to be considered bargains? Home buyers may surprise us all by freezing in their tracks and refusing to pay such "ridiculous" rates.

The good news is that 40 percent of homes that are owned have no mortgages at all, so rising rates will not be a factor for those homeowners. Also, Freddie Mac's chief economist Frank E. Nothaft observed that only one mortgage in seven had a coupon rate above 7 percent, which shows that most homeowners with mortgages have taken advantage of lower rates.

This could have an unexpected bull effect on the housing market. If high interest rates mean people stay put and do not move, housing prices could go up due to decreased inventory, and interest rates will not be as much of a deterrent for home buyers as economists might think. Why? Interest rates can always be refinanced, but one thing that cannot be changed is the sold price of the property.

According to the NAR, rising interest rates affect home price appreciation only to the extent that slowing sales may affect the supply/demand relationship. In other words, if slowing sales result in improving inventory levels—as we expect—it can bring supply closer to demand and take pressure off home prices. When a market is closer to equilibrium between buyers and sellers, multiple bids will become far less common and appreciation will cool to a more normal rate of growth.

The Roles of Fannie Mae and Freddie Mac

Fannie Mae and Freddie Mac are both privately held, despite their government charters, and are traded on the New York Stock Exchange and other exchanges. They are part of the S&P 500 Composite Stock

Price Index. Government-sponsored enterprises (GSEs), like Fannie Mae and Freddie Mac, are mandated to "make sure mortgage money is available for people in communities all across America." However, they do not lend money directly to home buyers. They do help lenders stay flush with mortgage funds.

For lenders to feel comfortable about lending, they have to have access to funds beyond the deposits their banking customers make. One way they do this is by making loans and then selling them on the secondary market. This creates the liquidity they need to relend that amount to the next borrower.

Incentives

Periodically, the government does things to encourage home ownership, such as raising conforming loan standards. Loans are said to "conform" when they meet the guidelines set to make them eligible for purchase by Freddie Mac or Fannie Mae. The purpose of this is to provide borrowers who meet conforming standards with the cheapest money possible and to give banks more liquidity so that they have more money to lend. If banks can sell their loans promptly on the secondary market, then they can turn around and make another loan to a new borrower. That allows more eligible people to buy homes.

Recently, the single-family mortgage loan limit for Fannie Mae and Freddie Mac rose to $417,000, which means more families can qualify for conforming loans in 2006. Second-mortgage loan limits will be $208,500, which should spur remodeling.

Most loans are well below the conforming limit, posing less risk for the nation's banks. The average loan size for single-family properties in the first three quarters of 2005 was about $172,000. Freddie Mac estimates that total mortgage interest savings for a borrower with a typical 30-year fixed-rate mortgage at the new conforming loan limit is as much as $24,700 over the life of the loan. This is certainly a good movement toward keeping mortgage money flowing.

THE UNDERPERFORMING STOCK MARKET

Another reason real estate has performed so well lately is that the stock market (at the time of this writing) remains well under its 2000 high. In 2006, Dr. Mark G. Dotzour, chief economist with the Real Estate Center at Texas A&M University, said that real estate property values are likely to continue to increase as long as the stock market continues to underperform. He believes that investors, faced with a low-yield environment, are choosing high-risk investments such as commodities trading, hedge funds, and even fine art. That is because it is a distressed investment environment where real estate looks attractive, even at inflated prices.

Stocks stagnate when sales cannot meet projections. If share prices are not growing, neither is an investor's portfolio. Investors want to see short-term as well as long-term gains. That puts tremendous pressure on companies to show growth every quarter.

EXPERT'S VIEW

"U.S. real estate sale prices increased more than 56 percent from the beginning of 1999 to the end of 2004, while the S&P index dipped nearly 6 percent..." But if you take the longer view, "you'll find that the S&P has actually stomped the real estate market, from Boston to Detroit to Dallas. From the start of 1980 to the end of 2004, home sale prices increased 247 percent. Over that same time period, however, the S&P 500 shot up more than 1,000 percent," wrote Sara Clemence of Forbes, on May 30, 2005.

Gains aside, stocks do not provide the real estate breaks that home-owners get from state and federal income tax incentives. As mutual funds, 401(k)s, and pension funds have lost money, average Joes are wondering why. Could it be that they do not know whom to trust when it comes to stocks?

Excessive CEO Compensation

CEO compensation is out of control. In 2000, it was 525 times the average worker's salary. After tech-wreck in 2001, salaries and options were more reasonable: 301 to 1. But by 2004, CEO compensation was sneaking back up to 431 to 1, says economists with the Institute for Policy Studies and United for a Fair Economy in their report, "Executive Excess, 2005." Today's CEO compensation is 10 times what it was in 1982, when the ratio was 42 to 1. If the average worker's compensation had kept pace, he or she would have made $110,136 instead of a paltry $27,460.

When American executives are making 78 times as much as the average worker, and more than 500 times as much when you throw in stock options, it is no wonder stocks are struggling to show a profit. Compared to German executives, who receive two-thirds less than American chiefs, and Japanese CEOs, who get by with only 16 times the average worker's paycheck, American executives appear unapologetically greedy and overpaid. Worse, unprecedented numbers have been caught cooking their own books to justify their inflated salaries and bonuses. A parade of high-level executives from publicly traded companies has gone before federal judges for investor fraud, causing many people to believe that investing in stocks is a carnie scam where the milk bottles are so leaded with concrete you could not knock them over with a cannonball.

A *New York Times* report on August 5, 2005, by Floyd Norris suggested that the stock options can actually encourage fraud. A study by Jared Harris and Philip Bromley, professors of management at the

University of Minnesota, found that companies granting large amounts of stock options were more likely to go broke and that "when those bosses received 92 percent or more of their pay in options, about 20 percent ended up cooking their books within five years."

The list of miscreants is long, from the stock analysts who promoted issues in which their investment banks had stakes to CEOs and staffers who lied to Wall Street and investors about their revenues. When tech-wreck occurred in 2001, angry investors began to scream for heads to roll, but they did not scream loudly enough.

Excessive CEO Severance Packages

Many corporate leaders are handsomely rewarded for driving their companies into the ground, raking in more money in severance packages than most people make in a lifetime. In 2003 it was reported that the average severance package for a CEO was $16.5 million, according to Paul Hodgson of The Corporate Library, a watchdog group. It's only gone up from there. Of the 367 firms Hodgson studied, 55.5 percent pay total salary, bonus, and equity awards for at least three years following the departure. His comment? "With CEOs receiving an average $15 million to start and $16.5 million to finish, they hardly need to make any money in between."

The bottom line is that smaller investors have been allowed to sit at the poor end of the banquet table thanks to lower brokerage fees, online trading, mutual funds, drip accounts, and more. But they've gotten such rotten leftovers, they're being poisoned.

When it comes to buying homes, at least investors have more control over what they are getting. There is some accountability to buyers through seller disclosures, E&O (errors and omissions) insurance by service providers, and other means. Sweetening the deal are borrowed money and tax incentives. When the average investor buys a share of stock, he or she has to pay for the share in full in advance. Any gains are taxable. With homes, the government is actively doing as much as possible to give borrowers money back and allowing them to keep most of the gains they make.

For many investors, that is a no-brainer. Why invest in the stock market where the "smartest guys in the room" show little or no respect for the shareholders? At least if a home loses value, the homeowner has somewhere to go to stew about it.

The McMansion: One Effect of the Housing Boom

One overlooked reason that houses have escalated so strongly in value is that they are being built larger than ever before—"super-sized." In 1950, the average new home housed 3.37 people in 983 square feet. By 2004, the average new home was 2,349 square feet, but thanks to divorce, delayed marriage, and easier loans for singles and single parents, these homes have only 2.60 occupants.

Why do we need so much more room? An October 2003 *Newsweek* article, "The McMansion Next Door" by Cathleen McGuigan, suggested that homebuilders are not making enough money, so they are super-sizing houses to attract the "bigger-must-be-better" home buyer. "Last year's annual report for Pulte Homes," said Ms. McGuigan, "one of the nation's biggest builders, contains an astonishing fact. If you adjust for inflation, houses of the same size and comparable features are the same price today as they were in the 1970s. That means that if business is going to grow, the industry has to sell more product—not just more houses, but more square footage."

Home designs always reflect the attitudes and affordability of the times. In the 1950s, after a world war had destroyed millions of homes and families, 1,000 feet seemed cozy and reassuring. It was not long before the wealthy 1950s gave way to a whopping 1,400 square feet. The ranch-style home became popular because back then we had lots of land to build on, so we spread out horizontally. We had big new cars and highway systems to take us to new destinations. Today, those low-slung homes have a charm of their own, and the land they occupy is worth more than the house that sits upon it.

EXAMPLE

In 1950, when homes were under 1,000 square feet, 86 percent were one story with two bedrooms or fewer and with 1½ baths. Fireplaces were a luxury enjoyed by only 20 percent of the homeowners. Over half of homes had no garage. Homes cost $11,000. Compare that to today's homes at over $200,000. By 1999, more than half of the homes had two stories and 2,225 square feet. The majority had three bedrooms, 2½ baths, one or more fireplaces, and two-car garages, and four out of five had central heat and air.

Flexible space is often requested by many families. Mom and Dad fly off to work at the same time—hence the need for lavish double baths with separate vanities, tubs, showers, and valet-appointed closets. That is a far cry from the 1950s, when Mom put on her pearls and made breakfast while Dad dressed for work. It was the kids who got the "big" bathroom because, back then, they were expected to share. Now sharing is viewed as punitive and invasive, with each resident deserving of a private bath, walk-in closet, and other amenities.

Working couples and parents want to interact with one another when they get home. The hidden kitchen has now become the "open," entertaining plan where "the cook of the day" can talk to whoever is in the family room or breakfast room. Even the lowly utility room has upsized into a multipurpose craft center, laundry, or mudroom, complete with sinks, second freezers, desks, tables, and storage.

We also need more and more room for our "stuff," as evidenced in the massive upsizing of closets, finished attics, "bonus rooms," and garages. While few families have three cars, they have enough sports gear, seasonal decorations, and lawn equipment to fill a three-car garage.

Even more interesting is how new homes are being built, with a majority of product designed for the nuclear family. Yet, intact mommy, daddy, two-kid families only constitute 25 percent of the market, if you go by U.S. Census Bureau households. If you go by the NAR, nearly half of home buyers have children under the age of 18.

While some of the contributors to the current housing market that are discussed in this chapter appear to be unrelated, each condition, such as government tax relief, is working in harmony with the other conditions to produce one of the most favorable and sustained home-buying markets in history.

The United States is experiencing an unprecedented period of government benevolence and subsidy toward home buyers and home-owners, where they receive incredible tax benefits and easy-to-get loans supplied by the liquidity provided by the secondary markets. Even the stock market is helping housing by failing to provide a safer haven for investment.

As long as these conditions continue, even if mortgage interest rates were to go up beyond 7 percent, home buying will still be attractive.

WHO'S BUYING AND WHO'S SELLING?

First-Time Home Buyers and How They Impact the Market

First-time home buyers are significant to the housing market because they herald the social and demographic changes that shape the future. These include changing family compositions and evolving housing preferences, which impact how housing is designed and built, as well as shifting mobility patterns that show where populations are likely to grow.

In 2005, first-time home buyers made up 40 percent of the market, about the same as in 2003 and 2004. This is a significant customer base for the "move-up" or repeat home buyer market. However, first-time home buyers do not necessarily buy "starter" homes, and repeat buyers are just as capable of scaling down as moving up, particularly as they age.

According to the NAR's 2005 Profile of Home Buyers and Sellers, the typical first-time home buyer is 32 years old, although 14 percent are under age 25. This can be compared to age 46, which is typical for repeat home buyers. First-time home buyers make less money than repeat home buyers—$57,200 compared to $83,200 (in 2005). Among all first-time home buyers, the chief reason for buying a home was to own a home of one's own, said four out of five (80 percent) of those surveyed by the NAR. Other reasons include the desire for more space (7 percent); new job (3 percent); and desire to be close to relatives, friends, and employment (3 percent).

The inaugural CENTURY 21® First-Time Home Buyer Index, November 2005, echoed the NAR's survey in the top reasons for buying a first home, which include the need for more room/space (36 percent), desire to build equity (24 percent), marriage (12 percent), need for privacy (10 percent), and job relocation (4 percent). The index offers some interesting contradictions because it mentions what buyers want in their dream homes in comparison to what they actually purchased.

DREAM HOMES

Not surprisingly, most of the CENTURY 21® respondents (78 percent) want a new home because new construction is "more appealing" to younger respondents (83 percent for those aged 18 to 34, compared to 68 percent for those aged 35 to 64). When imagining where their "dream home" would be located, more respondents preferred suburban areas (46 percent) to rural (39 percent) or urban (15 percent) somewhere in the southern United States. Most popular with home buyers was the Southeast, with 27 percent of the vote, followed closely by the Southwest at 23 percent. The Northeast (19 percent), Midwest (17 percent), and Northwest (14 percent) weren't as popular, with the exception of a few northern cities.

Yet they were not totally living in a dream world.

Respondents recognized that it would be a challenge to get into the home of their dreams. Almost two-thirds of the respondents (64 percent) believed it would take them more than five years to save the money needed to purchase their dream homes. Only 3 percent of respondents said they were already living in their dream homes. Specific reasons for the "ideal city" choice were:

- Friends and family members
- Reputation as a great city to raise a family (26 percent in part due to highly regarded school systems and low crime rates)
- Climate (22 percent)
- Proximity to water, sand, and mountains (22 percent)
- Strong local economy with many job opportunities (16 percent)

THE "REAL" FIRST-HOME PURCHASE

According to the survey respondents, the average length of time it took to find a first home was just over six months, with the quality of local schools a primary concern. Nearly half (48 percent) of the respondents expected to move out of their first homes in fewer than seven years.

In contrast to their dream homes:

- 73 percent of the first-time home buyers looked for resale homes.
- 27 percent sought out new construction.
- 78 percent of the respondents paid or expected to pay less than $250,000 for their first home, with the average home price being $215,000.
- 28 percent (over one-quarter of respondents) received help with the down payment from family members.
- 56 percent of the surveyed respondents planned to put down less than 20 percent of the home purchase price.

First-time home buyers are crucial to the real estate industry, because once they buy, they usually continue to buy. They make possible the move-up market for larger, more expensive homes, second homes, and investment homes.

Home-Buyer Demographics

With one birth every 7 seconds, one death every 14 seconds, and one immigrant arriving every 26 seconds, the U.S. population is adding one person every 10 seconds. That statistic alone should remove any thoughts of a housing bust, since builders cannot build much faster than they already are building because of the limitations of land, labor, and materials availability, as well as local bureaucratic roadblocks. And they certainly do not want to build more homes than the number of new households being formed to buy them.

Since builders do not like to pay interest on homes that are not selling, the building industry keeps a careful eye on what consumers are buying and what they say they want, as well as anticipating what consumers are going to want down the road based on demographics and consumer preferences. This enables developers and contractors to build toward the future so that they can anticipate which water feature to put in—a slide pool or therapy baths, or both.

Yet some feel there is more inventory than the country needs. The Center for Economic and Policy Research states that the "economy is building over 2 million housing units annually, while the number of households is growing by only about 1.4 million a year." However, somebody is buying these homes, since new homes are being absorbed at a rate that only leaves 4.7 months' worth of inventory on hand, as of this writing. When the absorption rate slows so do housing starts, so housing doesn't sit for long.

So who are these home buyers? They are a group diverse in age and ethnicities with highly individual lifestyle preferences that differentiate them, creating product development and marketing challenges for developers, builders, lenders, real estate professionals, and investors.

THE SPECIFIC GENERATIONS

Apart from their ages, the generations differ from one another in a number of ways. Their attitudes are formed according to a number of influences including socioeconomic events, the emergence of technologies and methods of communication, and geography, to name only a few. However, members of the same generation can also disagree politically, morally, and attitudinally—making them more like other generations than the one to which they belong.

The generations mentioned in this discussion will be limited to only those old enough to buy a home. According to Robert Wendover,

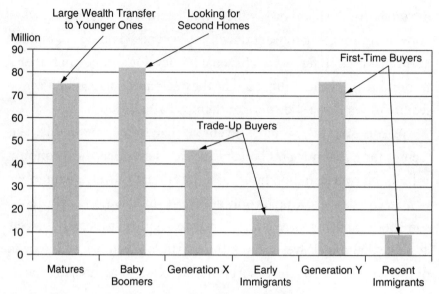

FIGURE 2.1 *Favorable Near-Term Demographic Trends*
Source: National Association of REALTORS®

Managing Director of the Center for Generational Studies, these home-buying generations can be roughly divided as follows:

- Matures (those born prior to 1946): 63 million
- Baby Boomers (born 1946 through 1964): 77 million
- Generation Xers (born 1965 through 1980): 50 million
- Generation Yers (born 1981 through 1999): 81 million

See Figure 2.1.

Matures

These home buyers cover the largest number of decades. "Matures" or "seniors" can be subdivided into the group that lived and served through the world wars and the group that was too young to serve. (See Figure 2.2.) As careful caretakers of their money, Matures tend to be sitting on a lot of equity and cash. Since they do not spend frivolously, they

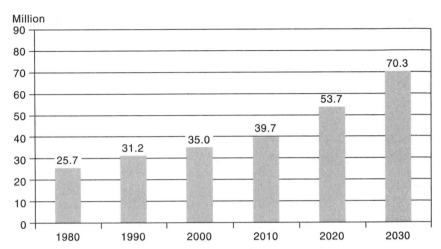

FIGURE 2.2 *Number of Persons Who Are 65+*
Source: U.S. Census Bureau

tend to be largely ignored by marketers, as well as developers, builders, and city planners (which is a mistake).

The GI Generation Born between 1901 and 1924, GIs were the first group to call themselves "senior citizens." These families are typically male-dominated, with long-term marriages. This hard-working group, who came of age during the Great Depression, tends to be careful with their money. They want experts in any area where they need help, so relationship-building is important to them. They tend to have lived in their homes for more than 30 years. They can be vulnerable to con games, so this makes them reluctant to make any changes without input from their grown children. As a result, they prefer their children to get involved in their housing decisions to make sure they are not being "taken for a ride."

The Silent Generation Born between 1925 and 1945, this is the only generation that has never been represented by someone their own age in the White House. As Depression babies, they were sandwiched between the duty-bound GI generation and the "me" generation called the Baby Boomers. They shouldered the Depression values of hard work and frugality. This generation is most interested in security and easy access to amenities and facilities such as medical centers and shopping. They are active, so they want to be near points of interest. If and when they downsize, they want access. They fear they may outlive their assets, and they do not want to be dependent on their children.

Matures as Home Buyers and Sellers Matures are in the autumn of their lives, a time in which they are selling or disposing of assets, not acquiring more. If and when they do buy, they want to be near family, friends, and activities. Many are willing to follow their Baby-Boomer and Gen-Xer children across the country.

Most have purchased several houses and have considerable experience with the whole process. You may find that many of these individuals use the houses they inspect while shopping for new residences as reference points to memories of previous homes. You might hear the wife say something like, "Our kitchen in Cleveland looked just like this." If she says it warmly, she may be picturing her kids sitting around the breakfast table. If she says it with derision, it may be reminding her of a bad experience. The couple may end up standing in the middle of the basement for 10 minutes telling a story that has come to mind because of the height of the ceiling, the brand of washer and dryer, or a variety of other stimuli. The key word for Matures is "memories."

Older home sellers have different concerns from younger sellers. About 41 percent of all home sellers are 55 or older. They have a lower median income than younger sellers, but when they sell, their homes net more cash—a median of $211,800—which can have significant tax and estate-planning consequences. When they repurchase, they tend to put down a lot more money, enabling them to buy either more expensive or second properties.

This helps to explain why nearly 68 percent of second-home buyers are over the age of 55.

In housing, they want security and access to medical and cultural facilities. Universal design utilizes such features as crank door handles, which are easier for arthritic hands to turn than doorknobs. It also includes single-floor homes with wider doorways for wheelchair access.

Baby Boomers

As the largest block of consumers in American history, Baby Boomers have been targeted by marketers since they were born, which makes it all the harder for them to give up the spotlight now. They were the first generation to use credit cards in a big way, which has also spilled over into their home-buying habits. Thanks to favorable tax laws, easy credit, and inherited wealth, Boomers are able to buy multiple properties—something previous generations could never do.

Boomers are also called the "sandwich" generation because some are still raising kids, taking responsibility for grandkids, housing grown children, or taking care of aging parents. Multigenerational households have been on the rise since 1970, and according to the most recent U.S. Census, there are 2.4 million grandparents taking primary caregiving responsibilities for their grandchildren.

Boomers want to believe that they are making the right decisions. But there can be many factors in this "right" decision. While most

Matures are at an age where appearances are not a large factor, many Boomers are still very much in the mode of "keeping up with the Joneses." Most are still actively involved with childrearing. The kids come first. "We must have a DSL connection so Johnny can use his computer," a father might say. "We also need a large garage to keep all the soccer and lacrosse equipment."

But not all are wealthy. Many are highly leveraged. They are willing to rack up enormous debt for convenience and appearance. Regardless of what has happened, they believe that "the sun will come out tomorrow."

While the majority of Boomers are parents, there are also a considerable number of childless couples in this generation who have chosen that lifestyle. The specific needs and desires of these individuals can vary widely.

Baby Boomers as Home Buyers and Sellers The Boomer generation contains an elite group that is able to purchase second homes, but this elite group can certainly not be generalized as the majority. While younger members are still active in the housing market, both older and younger Boomers are looking for convenience, time, luxury, and the latest gadget to impress their friends.

Buy now and pay later is still their mantra. Generally possessing more disposable income than their parents' generation, they have the wherewithal to purchase substantial homes in more affluent areas. But their sense of "curb appeal" may differ considerably, since some Boomer parents look for kid-oriented neighborhoods with lots of activities, while single Boomers tend to want communities near urban centers.

If builders and developers want to sell to them, they have to *make it about them*. Most Boomers have considerable experience purchasing homes and are clearly able to articulate what they want. With this generation presently in its peak house-buying years, it represents a solid opportunity for continued growth in the real estate industry.

Generation Xers

"The last half of the Boomer generation and the first half of the Generation X generation grew up during the chaos of the 1960s and early 1970s—a time of race riots, long lines to buy gasoline, Watergate, and the burning of bras and draft cards," explains John Ansbach, founder of the Generational Consulting Group and vice president of RECON, a strategic advisory firm to the real estate industry. "Growing up, their families were affected by massive corporate layoffs, recession, double-digit interest rates, the Iranian hostage crisis, the Challenger tragedy, and Three Mile Island." They are products of a 50 percent divorce rate, seesawing economies, and the collapse of government subsidies that resulted in poorer schools and declining neighborhoods.

Gen-Xers are the latch-key children who grew up feeling that the world that had been left to them is not a *better* place. Their disappointment in the husbandry of previous generations (particularly Boomers) colors their approach to problem solving. They rely on their own network of friends. When they want advice regarding the purchase of a big ticket item (like a car or home), they e-mail their 50 closest friends for their feedback. They trust peer opinions, while Boomers tend to trust legacy brand names.

Practicality is the watchword for this group. They are not as much into appearances and status as Boomers, preferring to create their own icons because they want speed, efficiency, and the ability to maintain balance in life. They are staying in school, marrying later, and having children later than any previous generation. They do not want to repeat the divorce rate of their parents. This is the generation that takes paternity leaves and will look for another job before risking the family's well-being for an 80-hour workweek.

They want information *now*, so they can make their own decisions. The babysitters for Gen-Xers were appliances, from television to handheld gaming devices. They were the first generation to get personal computers in schools, so they are very comfortable with technology. They are willing to spend money but are not ashamed of driving a hard bargain, such as asking real estate professionals to cut their fees.

They prefer to do business with contemporaries who know how to use the myriad of electronics they own. Information sharing is a strong characteristic of this generation. When you think of this generation, remember the communication tools that have been developed for them, such as laptops, Blackberries, and camera phones.

This is the generation that buys starter versions of luxury cars, and they do the same with housing. Gen-Xers are better educated than previous generations and armed with lots of money earned in high-paying jobs. With their superior electronic skills, they tend to want to do their own research. If Boomers are the "me" generation, then Gen-Xers are the "show me!" generation.

Gen-Xers as Home Buyers and Sellers Gen-Xers are the largest group of first-time home buyers. Since they distrust previous generations, they want their own rewards. This includes luxury amenities their parents could never have afforded, such as granite countertops in kitchens and spa tubs and rain showers in master baths.

They tend to want new housing and have little desire for homes that require maintenance or repairs. As singles, they tend to bypass the rent-until-you-settle-down phase, preferring to buy their own homes. After marriage, they may keep one home and rent the other, or they may sell both homes to acquire a larger or more expensive home.

They are likely to prepare for the home-buying experience with an organized list of expectations about school, location, pricing, and house features. When touring houses, they may use this same list as a reference point against which to compare. Generally speaking, they are the least likely of any generation to get swept up in the emotions of home buying, as they are likely to view home buying as an investment.

Generation Yers

Generation Y is otherwise known as Gen-Yers, Echo Boomers, and Millennials. This age group is larger in volume than the Baby Boomers, representing enormous possibilities of growth and change for the housing industry. As they enter their prime spending years, Gen-Yers are "ethnically diverse (38 percent are nonwhite), technologically savvy, accomplished multitaskers, and prolific consumers. In 2003, this generation spent $175 billion, including $22 billion on cell phones alone.

EXPERT'S VIEW

According to Pamela M. Hamilton, senior vice president at Centre City Development Corp. in San Diego, the housing needs of Generation Y are proving to be very different from those of their parents. Unlike many Baby Boomers, who tended to have children soon after college, members of Generation Y are postponing marriage and parenthood far longer, creating a "gap" period in which their lifestyles are often carryovers of their college days. Because their social interaction centers around nightlife rather than entertaining at home, they are satisfied with small, even tiny housing units in edgy locations.

This is the first generation to make less money than their parents because of corporate downsizing and more competition for jobs. For that reason, they are likely to live at home post-graduation and prefer living close to work, recreation, shopping, and entertainment. They place a high value on living in areas they perceive as offering a good quality of life. They seek diversity and new experiences and are the generation that is most comfortable making and having friends of all ages and all backgrounds.

Gen-Yers will see more change in communications and purchase power than the Boomers ever dreamed of. They have already changed music and music-sharing with Napster and iPods; journalism with *blogs*. They are device-dependent, meaning they are less likely to have answers in their heads; however, they retain an almost photographic memory for where to find information and answers.

As strategist and futurist Kathy Lamancusa observed in 2000, "Never before has a generation been as independent or had as much influence as Generation Y. . . . Teenagers today are defined by time and money or, more specifically, their parents' lack of time and abundance of money," writes Lamancusa. "In a majority of cases, both parents work outside the home, leaving Generation Y to become more self-sufficient and more mature at an earlier age than previous generations. Parents now treat their kids as near equals and give their opinions considerable weight. This means Generation Y has a direct input on every purchase that is family-oriented, including houses and cars."

Gen-Yers as Home Buyers and Sellers Currently, many Gen-Yers can afford homes because rental properties are being converted to condominiums. In addition, current loan products favor low down payments and favorable terms, allowing them to get into housing earlier than previous generations. As first-time home buyers, Gen-Yers are likely to be getting financial help and support from parents and other family members. Builders and Realtors are surprised to find their clients are still in college or recently graduated.

As housing becomes more expensive, look for Gen-Yers to return to their sharing roots. The housing industry will design "communal" rather than community living, with common living rooms, media rooms, and outdoor space, as well as increased opportunities for singles, nontraditional couples, roommates, and families to become home buyers through rent-to-buy options.

Selling or renting to this generation requires lots of photos, maps, statistics, and points of interest so that the Millennials can share this information with family and friends and make decisions when they are comfortable.

Generation Y likes to be entertained with eye and ear candy, but they also care deeply about the preservation of the environment. Think green. This is one group that is more impressed with energy-saving rather than stainless steel appliances.

Immigration and Cultural Diversity

Minority households are growing. Between 1991 and 2003, they increased from 22 to 35 percent. New-home buyers increased from 13 to 24 percent and home remodelers from 12 to 19 percent.

This has the housing industry salivating.

U.S. Census figures from 2004 tell us that the majority of whites are homeowners (75.7 percent), but African Americans, Hispanics, Asians, and others are catching up, creating an exciting opportunity for minority investors.

Minority home ownership is on the rise due to the government's recognition of the need to help these buyers with educational programs and other assistance to become homeowners. For example, between 1993 and 2002, Fannie Mae's overall mortgage financing for African Americans increased by 323 percent, while the number of African American households it served rose by 220 percent.

DISCRIMINATION IN HOME OWNERSHIP

However, the government has to watch out for predatory lenders who take advantage of recent immigrants and minorities. These two groups "will make up the bulk of new households and about half of the first-time home buyers in the coming decades," said *USA Today* (December 2004). They are "far more likely than whites to take out sub-prime loans—and appear more likely to be victimized by predatory lending."

In 2000, Housing and Urban Development (HUD) and The Urban Institute conducted surveys and found that in metropolitan sales markets, "African American home buyers—like renters—continue to face discrimination. Specifically, white home buyers were more likely to be able to inspect available homes and to be shown homes in more predominantly white neighborhoods than were black home buyers. In addition, whites also received more information and assistance with financing than comparable black home buyers."

"Hispanic home buyers also face significant levels of discrimination," said the report. "Non-Hispanic whites were consistently favored in 19.7 percent of tests. In particular, non-Hispanic whites were more likely to receive information and assistance with financing and to be shown homes in non-Hispanic neighborhoods than comparable Hispanic home buyers."

Immigrants also face hurdles. According to the Center for Housing Policy's "Housing Landscape for America's Working Families, 2005," critical housing needs are greater for immigrants and native-born Americans, with the disparity being the highest in the Northeast where immigrants have almost one and a half times the critical housing needs of native-borns.

Majority Minority

The Fair Housing Act makes it unlawful to discriminate based on race, color, national origin, religion, sex, familial status, or handicap (disability). Hopefully, with a little time, discrimination will take care of itself, as the nation is headed toward a majority minority.

Texas, California, New Mexico, and Hawaii are already majority-minority states, and Maryland, Georgia, Mississippi, and Arizona are headed that way too. While some may resist the change, the fact is that in the next 20 to 30 years, the American population will be majority minority—a true melting pot. (See Figure 2.3.)

However, the current wave of immigration that started in the early 1990s is mostly from Asia and Latin America. Millions of immigrant

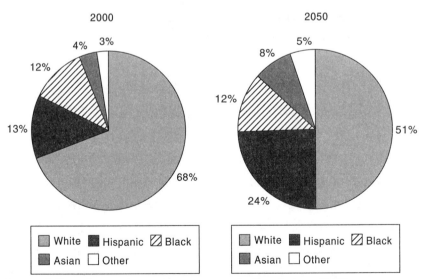

FIGURE 2.3 *The Population of 2000 versus the Population of 2050*
Source: U.S. Census Bureau

49

buying patterns are undocumented and could cause significant demographic shifts. A study of 1990 and 2000 U.S. Census data by Gary Painter and Zhou Yu of the University of Southern California's Lusk Center for Real Estate suggests that younger immigrants are more likely to own homes than United States–born counterparts, but affordability is an issue. Immigrant working families are nearly 70 percent more likely than native-born Americans to spend more than half their income on housing and six times more likely to live in crowded conditions than native-born Americans.

That means many can't afford to buy, according to "America's Newest Working Families: Cost, Crowding, and Conditions for Immigrants," by the National Housing Conference's (NHC) research affiliate, the Center for Housing Policy. These working families are defined as low- to moderate-income families working the equivalent of full-time jobs and earning between the full-time minimum wage of $10,712 and up to 120 percent of the median income in their areas.

Minorities will account for an estimated two-thirds of new households over the next 10 years. By 2010, half of the first-time home buyers will be minorities, when nearly 3 in 10 households will be headed by a minority.

Real Estate Investors and Second-Home Buyers

The current real estate market is attracting all sorts of investors—short- and long-term—and some of them are not being quite honest about the intended use of the home they are buying. Whether they are hoping for homestead status or trying to get a better loan rate, the number of people buying real estate with no intention of occupying the houses is on the rise. (See Figure 2.4.)

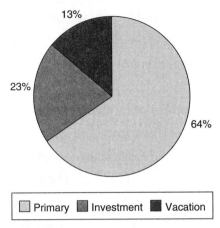

FIGURE 2.4 *Second-Home Buying on the Rise*
Source: National Association of REALTORS®

One-third of the homes purchased in 2004 and four out of five homes purchased in 2005 were second homes or investments. Yet, in NAR's 2004 profile of home buyers and sellers, the association found that, out of the home buyers they surveyed, 97 percent purchased property they intended to use as their homes, while 1 percent purchased vacation homes and 2 percent purchased investment properties. Later, a new study published in March 2005 found that investment property and vacation homes made up a "significant portion of the overall housing market, accounting for more than one-third of residential transactions," according to NAR. The reason for the gap is all in the semantics. Just because you only plan to occupy a home for a little while does not mean it is not an investment. This brings us to a new era: the day-trader home-buyer market.

How did we go from 3 percent to 33.3 percent?
Easy. Home buyers can't be trusted in surveys.

The strength of the second-home market was not only unanticipated, it cannot even be accurately tracked. The NAR had excellent results from studies looking at owner-occupied homes, but had no methodology to determine the representative market share for vacation and investment homes, or how many individual owners owned more than one vacation or investment property.

Previous studies indicated that the total stock of second homes purchased for investment or recreation was about 6.6 million units, with the lion's share earmarked as vacation homes. However, there has been a significant shift over the last few years with a growing number of second-home buyers purchasing primarily for investment and not recreation.

According to U.S. Census data from 2003, there are 43.8 million second homes in the United States, including 6.6 million vacation homes and 37.2 million investment units, compared with 72.1 million owner-occupied homes, and that's the latest data available, although it's likely that second-home buyers are buying more investment property than vacation homes.

"In essence, our definition of second homes has changed with the buyer shift toward investment property," says David Lereah, chief economist for the NAR. "In examining Census data to determine the number of investment units, we see that second homes are a much larger share than the conventional mindset of them being mostly vacation homes." If one-third of the homes purchased in 2004 were second homes, how many were vacation homes and how many were investments? We do not know.

However, according to NAR research into the second-home buyer market, we do know that:

- Median vacation home buyers are 55 years old with a total household income of $71,000.
- Median investment-property home buyers are 47 years old with a total household income of $85,700.

- More than half of investment-property home buyers spend no time in their second homes.
- Eighty-six percent of vacation-home buyers do not rent out their vacation homes.
- The median distance between a vacation-home buyer's primary residence and second home is 49 miles, and it costs $190,000.
- The median distance between an investment-property buyer's primary residence and second home is 18 miles, and it costs $148,000.
- Nearly one-half of the second-home buyers used their savings for a down payment.

FLIPPERS AND SPECULATORS

Flipping has generally referred to the practice of acquiring real estate at substantially less than the market value and reselling it quickly at full market value. Loans repaid quickly are often subject to a prepayment penalty, and property sold within two years of acquisition is usually subject to capital gains taxes. This is why most home buyers intend to stay or do stay longer than the two years required: to skip capital gains taxes up to $250,000 for singles and $500,000 for couples. Most home buyers wait about seven years before they get the itch to move, but some cannot resist that get-rich-quick promise in real estate.

The key to flipping is turning the property at the right time—90 to 180 days, according to a report by First American Residential Solutions.

But that's the trick, isn't it—knowing when to hold 'em, fold 'em, walk away, run?

But flipping has a narrow window of success, which means timing the market to buy while a property is distressed but in a healthy enough market that it can be turned quickly. That means that poor economies with lots of job loss aren't a good bet, because there's no momentum for growth. Instead, a flipper must scavenge in a healthy market for bargains—foreclosures, distress sales, fixer-uppers, or new construction.

In extremely hot markets, it has become unnecessary even to move in or get a renter at all. A new kind of speculator buys a home, presold by the builder, well before construction begins. Before completion, he or she sells the home to another buyer, often using the builder as a mediator. Builders are willing to help in some cases because they can sell substantial upgrades to the new buyer, thus upping their profits. Working with flippers also allows builders to have a backup plan in case the original contract falls through. This has occurred in some Las Vegas and southern Florida markets, where real estate has been so hot that buyers have been willing to endure long lines and lotteries to get into homes in specific communities.

Experts predict that the second-home market will stay strong as long as Boomers are still in their peak earning years. According to the NAR, 92 percent of all second-home buyers see their property as a good investment. In addition, 38 percent say it is very likely they would purchase another home within two years.

CHAPTER 3

WHY AND WHERE DO PEOPLE BUY HOMES?

Choosing a Home

All homeowners or speculators want to know if they are making a good investment and that their property can be easily sold or leased. They do not buy to lose money, but they also do not necessarily buy to make a lot of money. In fact, the evidence points to quality of life as the primary reason people buy homes.

QUALITY OF LIFE

According to the NAR's most recent survey of buyers and sellers, home buyers chose their new home for a variety of reasons:

- Good neighborhoods (68 percent)

- Close to jobs/school (43 percent)
- Specific school district (23 percent)
- Close to family and friends (36 percent)
- Close to shopping (19 percent)
- Close to parks/recreation (17 percent)
- Planned community (11 percent)
- Near entertainment venues (7 percent)
- Near airports (6 percent)
- Near health facilities (6 percent)
- Near public transportation (6 percent)
- Other (18 percent)

As you can see, making money is not mentioned on the list, but could be thrown into the category "other" (18 percent). However, outlined clearly are the quality of life issues.

Neighborhood preferences are dictated by the location of homes that contribute to quality of life issues. Suburban home buyers were the most likely to be concerned about schools, while small-town buyers wanted to be near friends and family. Urban home buyers were most interested in short commutes and access to shopping, entertainment, and public transportation. Whatever home buyers' preferences, quality of life seems to be at the top of the list.

INVESTMENT OPPORTUNITIES

One-third of the 2004 through 2005 home buyers were reputedly second-home and investment buyers—not primary-home buyers. Do investors buy for quality of life or for profit? Second-home buyers, according to NAR research, spent 9 percent more on their homes than those who purchased their homes as primary residences. Sixty-eight percent of second-home buyers bought single-family homes—fewer than primary-home buyers—but they bought more duplexes and condos (presumably for a quality of life where the homeowner's association handles most upkeep and repairs). Most investors (21 percent) spent less than $100,000, while another extreme (14 percent) spent more than $500,000. This shows that investments largely trend toward the extremes: workforce or entry-level housing and its opposite, luxury housing.

In general, the trick to making a good housing investment is buying right in the first place. For buy-and-hold investors, the trick is learning what people are going to want in housing down the road. While this can be done by watching trends, demographic shifts and economic growth, there are five specific keys to making a good home investment:

1. *Location*—owning property in a location where other people want to live
2. *Appreciation*—owning the right kind of property for the times
3. *Condition*—keeping the home updated and repaired
4. *Timing*—buying low and selling high; buyers' versus sellers' markets
5. *Negotiation*—paying and getting the price you want

Where Do People Move?

The U.S. population will increase by 10 percent by the end of this decade. However, there are only three ways states can grow: (1) more births than deaths, (2) immigration from other countries, and (3) in-migration from other states. (See Figures 3.1 and 3.2.)

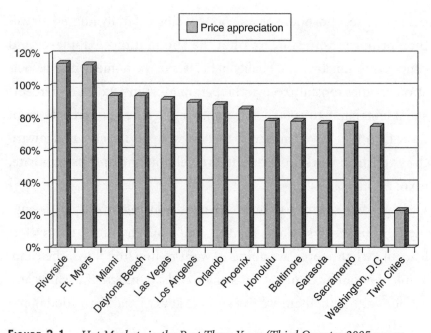

FIGURE 3.1 *Hot Markets in the Past Three Years (Third Quarter 2005 versus Third Quarter 2002)*
Source: National Association of REALTORS®

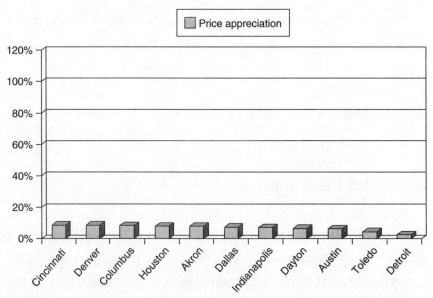

FIGURE 3.2 *Cool Markets in the Past Three Years (Third Quarter 2005 versus Third Quarter 2002)*
Source: National Association of REALTORS®

CRISSCROSS MIGRATION PATTERNS

In its report *Domestic Migration across Regions, Divisions, and States, 1995–2000*, released August 2003, the U.S. Census Bureau found that some interesting patterns were developing. Over 22 million people changed their states of residence, and half of those relocated to states outside of their home states' region. This has created a crisscross migration pattern the likes of which our country has not seen since Horace Greeley advised young men to "Go West" over a century ago.

Before we go further, let's be sure we're talking apples to apples.

According to the U.S. Census Bureau definitions:

- *Migration* refers to moves that cross state, division, or regional jurisdictional boundaries.
- *In-migration* is migration into an area for a certain period of time.
- *Out-migration* is migration out of an area for a certain period of time.
- *Net migration* is the difference between immigration and out-migration in a given area during a specific period of time.
- *Gross migration* is the sum of immigration and out-migration in a given area during a specific period of time.

Examples of these growth patterns can be seen with such states as Nevada. It has been the fastest-growing state for the past 18 years. It had the highest net migration of all the states, with a gain of 151.5 people for every 1,000 residents in 1995. California had the highest gross migration, exceeding 3.6 million between 1995 and 2000, yet, *out-migration* exceeded *in-migration* by 756,000 people. (See Table 3.1.)

U.S. MIGRATION TREND
Top Five versus Bottom Five

State	Net Migration from 2000 to 2003 (in thousands)
Florida	+541
Arizona	+194
Nevada	+146
Georgia	+140
North Carolina	+108
Massachusetts	−102
Ohio	−103
Illinois	−238
California	−277
New York	−551

TABLE 3.1
Source: U.S. Census Bureau

As far as trends go, the states of Nevada and Arizona had the most net migration. The South as a region had the most net migration, particularly in the states of Florida, Georgia, and North Carolina. Hmm . . . there are some interesting reversal of fortunes for states like California and New York, which are seeing the out-migration of their populations to greener pastures.

This trend suggests that the Northeast and Midwest will be out-populated by the South by the year 2010. More residents will live in Florida than in New York in fewer than five years, and North Carolina will out-populate New Jersey in fewer than three years. For the first time, Massachusetts has lost residents, as did Ohio, Michigan, West Virginia, Connecticut, and Maryland, which suggests a seismic population shift from densely populated Eastern cities to warmer, less-crowded Southern and Western states.

Although today California remains the most populated state at 35.9 million people, it continues to lose more residents to other states than it gains. Its population growth is primarily a result of foreign immigration.

CITY GROWTH

Thirty-six of the nation's 84 largest cities that lost population in the 1970s saw a turnaround in the 1980s and 1990s. Enjoying an urban renaissance were New York City, Portland (Oregon), Providence, San Francisco, Fort Worth, Indianapolis, and Tampa. Also regaining population were Atlanta, Chicago, Denver, and Minneapolis.

Building has not always kept up with demand. In the 1980s, unusually favorable tax treatments encouraged a wave of multifamily rental construction that subsided by the 1990s. A percentage of that inventory has been reclaimed and rehabbed as condos, causing a dearth of affordable rental housing.

Can you say opportunity?

Urban renewal—the rehabilitation of older, abandoned, or distressed city center areas—consists mostly of tearing down older properties and putting up new commercial venues. This construction generally brings in more tax dollars to city coffers, because the strongest construction is between 5 and 20 miles from core business districts.

City growth has included about 18 million new homes over the last decade, but the distribution of those homes has been fairly uneven, favoring Southern and Western cities while Northern and Midwestern areas lost population. Among the areas with the most construction permits between 1994 and 2003 were Southern California (Orange County, San Diego), Dallas-Fort Worth, Houston, Phoenix, Las Vegas, northwest Colorado, Florida (Orlando, Naples), Chicagoland (greater Chicago area), and New York and Boston.

Housing Characteristics

No discussion of where people want to live would be complete without exploring what kinds of housing people want. Once a year, the NAR does a survey to see how many of the homes that were purchased were new, as compared to existing ones. According to the 2005 Profile of Home Buyers and Sellers, the majority of home buyers (77 percent) purchased existing homes, while 23 percent bought new construction. In 2003, more home buyers (28 percent) bought new homes, which suggested that new housing would be a trend, but percentages returned to norms (around 20 percent or one-fifth of homes sold are new homes) by 2005.

Seventy-five percent bought single-family detached homes, down from 79 percent in 2003. Single-family, detached housing is typically the most expensive, which is why repeat home buyers (79 percent) are more likely to buy them than first-time home buyers (69 percent). Nine percent purchased a row house or townhouse (homes with attached walls usually separated by a firewall), and the remainder bought duplexes or some other form of multifamily housing.

Once again there was proof that real estate market conditions are local, the most densely populated part of the country is the Northeast, so it isn't surprising that more townhomes/rowhomes were sold there than in the Midwest. In the South, where home building has been setting new records, 25 percent of the homes sold were new, while 75 percent were existing homes.

DIVERSITY IN HOUSING LIFESTYLE

Along with diversity in population come diversity in lifestyles and the resulting housing choices. Thanks to the burgeoning condo market, buyers can be more relaxed about the type of home they buy without worrying whether or not it will appeal to a certain demographic. In fact, nontraditional households are the norm, and marrieds-with-children are the new minority—about 25 percent of the population, but a majority minority of home buyers. This demographic reversal should be causing developers, builders, and interior designers to rethink what makes a livable home. Instead of moving out to the suburbs and catering only to the single-family-home-with-a-yard home buyers, builders are beginning to experiment with a variety of housing styles, from trendy lofts with young singles in mind to senior-focused communities filled with age-friendly amenities like walking trails and exercise/therapy pools.

Parents with children are still perceived as the ideal first-time-buyer segment that can be turned into happy repeat buyers, even though other types of buyers may actually be better prospects. For example, more people under the age of 25 are buying homes than ever before, and many are single. Homeowners younger than 25 have doubled over the last 10 years to 1.64 million from 807,000. However, as first-time home buyers, they can afford less for their first home ($150,000) than a repeat buyer ($235,000).

Condominiums

Between 1995 and 2003, the number of occupied condos climbed by more than one-fifth from 4.4 million to 5.4 million, according to the Joint Center for Housing Studies. Consequently, starts of multifamily condos jumped from 71,000 in 2003 to 121,000 in 2004. Buyers are pouring into condominiums, presumably for the lock-and-go, low-maintenance lifestyle they promote. *American Demographics* recently reported that condominium prices have risen above those of single-family homes. From September 2004 to September 2005, condo prices shot up 9 percent to $213,600. Clearly, people are not buying them because they are cheaper.

Pam O'Connor, CEO of Leading Real Estate Companies of the World, says there are several reasons condo sales are up: their versatility as vacation/event homes, commuter homes, college campus substitute housing, pieds-a-terre, and investments. In addition, condominiums are ideal properties for the "mixed-use" trend in city planning and redevelopment—the concept that people can live and work in the same area, walk to the grocery and park, and generally build a neighborhood that is supported by both commercial and residential interests. "The flow of capital into commercial real estate is at an unprecedented level, with multifamily transactions accounting for about a third of the total," said NAR's chief economist David Lereah. Purchases of multifamily property rose 90 percent in 2005.

Driving the boom in condos are older singles or empty-nesters, who are buying in the 20 highest-cost metros. Also, first-time home buyers, 9.1 percent of whom purchased condos since 1999, as opposed to only 7.3 percent of trade-up buyers, are going for the low-maintenance lifestyle. However, builders may not be reacting quickly enough. Well over 95 percent of homes are created for the ambulatory, yet rapidly aging Boomers will still be the majority of home buyers and homeowners for years to come. Households with owners aged 55 to 74 will increase 36 percent through 2015. As a result, homes with "universal features" like single-story floor plans, wide doorways, easy-to-use door handles, etc. will be in greater demand than the oversized, two-story McMansion on small yards that are in demand today.

THE NONTRADITIONAL BUYER

Once considered the perfect family and the target-market ideal, the nuclear family—consisting of mother, father, a boy child, and a girl child—constituted the largest home-buying demographic in 1998, a whopping 64 percent of the market. Yet that number is falling annually, to less than 50 percent in 2005. It is the nontraditional buyer who is changing the dynamics of the real estate market. This means that the industry has to gain knowledge not just about families with children and their needs, but about the attitudes and needs of all kinds of nontraditional home buyers.

Many in this market segment come under Fair Housing protection, so their needs must also be met. Nonwhite racial and ethnic buyers are a growing segment of the housing market. Although whites made up 90 percent of the home-buying market in 1998, blacks accounted for 5 percent. About 8 percent of the white market was made up of Latinos, Spanish, or Hispanics. Their home-buying goals and attitudes may differ greatly from those of whites. Some ethnicities will not incur debt, even to buy a house, so the way they are accommodated by the industry is very different from the way debt-loving whites are treated.

Single women made up 18 percent of transactions, with single men accounting for 11 percent. Unmarried couples and others accounted for 7 percent of all sales. Three out of 10 households were maintained by women with no husband present. According to the U.S. Census Bureau, only 25 percent of the households had children under the age of 18. And the number of married couples with no children is expected to grow by 7 million by the year 2010.

Households are smaller, but their number is growing. The average number of people occupying individual households is down to 2.65 from 3.14 in 1970. The number of family households is projected to increase by 15 percent by 2010, adding more than half the growth of total households. These households will be increasingly occupied by childless couples, single-parent families, and people living alone.

Many cities, particularly in the South, are already seeing a countertrend developing. Instead of flocking to the suburbs for housing, many home buyers, particularly from the nontraditional segment, are deliberately seeking the hustle and bustle of downtown and city environments. This trend is opening up new home environments, including warehouse district lofts and high-rise residential buildings consisting of both condominiums and apartments. Townhomes and zero-lot lines are also making a comeback. What this means is that the market for larger homes may well reverse itself. As the small household takes a larger share in demographics, the market for large suburban homes may well dry up.

Why is this happening? The nontraditional buyer has different concerns than the white, nuclear family and increasingly has the buying power to own a home and establish a lifestyle of his or her own. Ethnic groups and alternative lifestyle groups tend to live near one another more than ever, despite inroads made toward integration in schools and the workplace. Communities can have distinct borders between countries of origin and lifestyle preference. Although blending in the workplace and schools are encouraged, people are choosing to keep their private life segregated.

The point is that for every trend, there is also a countertrend, and new communities will increasingly show more diversity in housing. That is why many developers are beginning to diversify with multiple styles of housing within the same master-planned communities. More frequently, you see apartments, townhomes, patio homes, and McMansions as the variety of offerings within the same community, where all ages and all types of families can live together comfortably.

New-Home Projections

In its America's Housing Projection for 2010, the National Association of Home Builders reported that housing will look approximately the same as it does now, but with a few more amenities. Count yourself ahead of the game if your home and property have the following features:

- 2,200 or more square feet
- Three or more bedrooms
- Two and a half bathrooms
- Garage for two or more cars
- Energy-efficient heating and cooling systems
- More steel, concrete, engineered wood, and recycled products
- Convertible interior designs to appeal to a variety of home buyers
- High-speed data access, modular wiring and controls, and multiple phone lines
- Security systems
- Neighborhoods with smaller lots, narrower streets, and less pavement
- More mixed-use communities
- $270,000–$280,000 price tag

CHAPTER
4

BUSTS—WHERE, WHY, AND WHEN

Can a Bust Be Defined?

If U.S. home prices have boomed in recent years—up almost 50 percent over the last five years—does that mean we are in a housing boom that is headed for a bust? According to the Federal Deposit Insurance Company (FDIC), sales have surpassed every increase of the last 25 years. However, most U.S. cities have demonstrated fairly stable home-price trends over time, with only 20 percent of 361 cities experiencing either a boom or a bust.

While others' definitions may differ, the FDIC defines a *boom* as a 30 percent or greater increase in inflation-adjusted (or real) home prices during any three-year period. A *bust,* then, is simply a reverse of the criteria—30 percent declines or greater within a three-year period. However, a more reasonable guideline, notes the FDIC, would be an "average decline in nominal home prices of at least 15 percent over five years or a nominal *15 in 5 rule.*" Since 1978, 63 different U.S. metropolitan areas have experienced at least one boom, and 24 of these metropolitan areas have experienced *more* than one. These booms (70 percent of the 63 markets) are concentrated in California and the Northeast. Conversely, 142 metro areas declined by at least 15 percent over a five-year period.

At this point in the report, the FDIC second-guesses itself, which goes to show that even experts use subjective criteria to determine market booms and busts. "Is the *15 in 5* guideline too lenient, resulting in too many cities being identified as declining?" ponder the FDIC researchers. "After all, what we are really saying is that the value of the average owner's home in these 142 metro areas simply failed to keep up with inflation during the five-year period and fell behind inflation by at least 15 percent." In other words, the price of the home in nominal terms may never have fallen at all.

The report explained that a period of "true distress" for homeowners and lenders might be better defined in terms of a large decline in nominal prices that push the value of properties below what homeowners owe on their mortgages. If homeowners had to sell in this type of situation, they would have to bring money to the closing table.

Stagnation or Bust?

Prior to 1998, in just 9 of 54 booms (about 17 percent), a bust occurred within five years of a boom, suggesting that stagnation in home prices is more likely to be an outcome of booms rather than busts. What is more likely to cause busts is distress experienced by the homeowners. To find the reasons, the FDIC explored two case studies involving the "oil patch" states of the mid-1980s and the bicoastal collapse of the 1990s.

Economic Shock and Real Estate Busts

When oil prices surged in the late 1970s, the oil-producing areas of Texas, Oklahoma, Louisiana, Colorado, Wyoming, and Alaska began experiencing an economic boom and population inflows. As the economies in these cities accelerated and their populations surged, demand for housing naturally boomed. In addition, cities such as Houston and San Antonio were reporting double-digit home price appreciation.

Crude oil prices surged 250 percent between 1978 and 1980 and then began a six-year decline, culminating in a 46 percent price drop in 1986. Gains began unraveling in 1983, with job loss and population outflows. The worst home price drops occurred in Lafayette, Louisiana (40 percent), and Casper, Wyoming (33 percent), between 1983 and 1988. By 1987, desperation was rampant. Anchorage lost 2 percent of its residents; Odessa-Midland's population dropped 5.4 percent; and Casper lost 7 percent of its residents. (Population outflows are deadly to housing markets because inventories increase and buyers are not available.)

The busts in California and the Northeast also had elements of distress, including the early 1990s recession, massive defense downsizing, and a commercial real estate collapse. Areas of the Northeast began a sharp downturn, with population losses to the Sunbelt states as people left the Rustbelt (states with automotive and steel-based economies, such as Michigan, Pennsylvania, and Ohio) to find jobs.

The obvious conclusion is that economic distress causes housing busts—not prior real estate booms. However, the longer and higher home prices rise, the more likely they are to escape the surly bonds of reason.

Current Risk Factors That Threaten the Housing Market

Changing job markets, rising interest rates, government and financial press interference, and the whims of the home-buying public are only a few of the most volatile influences on home prices. Others include glut of housing inventories, overspending for homes relative to income, high-risk loans, unemployment, the drumbeat of the negative financial press, lack of affordability, foreclosures, mortgage fraud, and debt addiction, to name only a few.

HOUSING GLUT

By January 2006, builders and real estate professionals were worried that housing inventories were growing too fast. Existing home sales had dropped for five months consecutively, even while home prices continued a double-digit climb. The U.S. Census Bureau reported that new homes sold at an annual rate of 1.23 million homes in January, down from 1.3 million sold in December 2005.

Home builders reported an increasing number of canceled new home orders. A survey by the National Association of Home Builders said that one in five members were reporting more cancellations than six months ago, and 4 percent of the home builders surveyed said the increase in cancellations had been significant.

Typically, new home cancellations can be explained by job loss. If job growth slows or people feel in jeopardy of losing their jobs, they will tend to back away from high-ticket purchases, such as homes, cars, and appliances. However, the home builders found that only 15 percent of the home buyers who canceled their contracts cited job loss as the cause. Forty-five percent of home buyers said their cancellations were due to an inability to sell their existing homes. One-third said they were not able to qualify for financing because of rising mortgage rates.

NAHB Chief Economist David Seiders and others believe there is another reason for cancellations that was not included in the survey: real estate investors who were ordering new homes with the intention of selling them quickly in a hot real estate market started to pull out of the real estate market. If speculators pull out of the new home market, is demand still strong with home buyers who intend to occupy their homes? Home buyers intending to live in a home are reluctant to cancel an order, even if the market seems to have softened. However, speculators will gladly leave deposits on the table if they think they will make more money by walking away from the investment. The exit of any large number of buyers is going to have a negative impact on the market—driving home prices downward.

EXPERT'S VIEW

"If you've overbuilt the market and sales get canceled, you have to do something with the homes," said David Seiders, chief economist of NAHB. "Builders are offering incentives that are already designed to support prices and stop cancellations."

New home supplies reached 5.2 months of inventory on hand in January 2005. That means it will take approximately 5 months to sell through existing inventories to zero homes on hand. New home builders are quick to slow down building new homes in order to let standing inventory get absorbed by the marketplace, so absorption should be fairly quick. If home cancellations continue and new orders

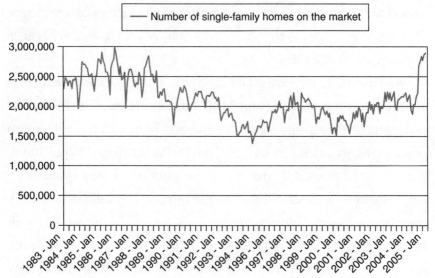

FIGURE 4.1 *Rising Existing Housing Inventory*
Source: National Association of REALTORS®

don't pick up again, then home builders will have reason to worry. On the other hand, if the slowdown is only temporary, another housing boom could be triggered, particularly if there is nowhere else investors prefer to put their money. (See Figure 4.1.)

An oversupply of homes can hurt, but thanks to a few hurricanes provided by Mother Nature and some overheated housing regions, the national housing market is not in oversupply yet. However, some economists worry that the population is only growing by about a million and a half households a year, while we are building 2 million homes a year.

According to "The Housing Bubble Fact Sheet," a white paper produced by the Center for Economic and Policy Research, housing construction "is equal to approximately 5 percent of the gross domestic product." Dean Baker, codirector for the Center, suggests that with home construction at a record high for the last several years, construction could fall back by as much as 40 percent, as it did in the

1981 to 1982 recession—a loss that would equal 2 percentage points of the gross domestic product.

Meanwhile, builders say they are building to demand. While housing starts slowed for July 2005, building permits for single-family homes rose a record 2 percent to an annual rate of 1.7 million. The Commerce Department says home construction has been boosted by strong sales, rising incomes, and appreciating home values.

Month-to-month swings in starts and permits data may not be meaningful. It is far better to look for trends to establish themselves over a period of several months. If you look at housing starts over the last five months, they are below 2 million, which should make some housing bubble–blowers breathe a little easier. In addition, new houses are being snapped up by buyers at record rates. In 2004, buyers purchased 1.2 million new homes and were on fire to do the same in 2005. (See Figure 4.2.)

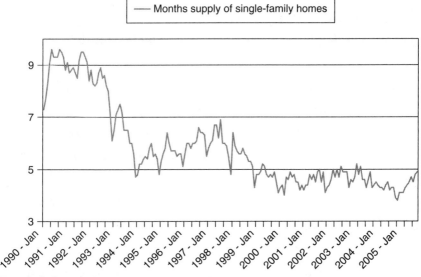

Figure 4.2 *Loosening Supply, Certainly Not an Oversupply*
Source: National Association of REALTORS®

In June 2005, more new houses were sold than ever before in a single month, leaving new home inventories at about a four-month supply. In more balanced markets, housing can swell to as much as six months on hand without causing any worries.

By year-end 2005, the median price of *new homes* was about $214,800—15 percent higher than in 2004. That was about the same rate of appreciation as *existing homes* were showing. According to the National Association of REALTORS®, existing home prices are at $219,000. Even though housing prices are projected to fall through the end of 2006, homeowners should still enjoy 5 to 10 percent gains in valuations, well above anticipated inflation rates.

During the last recession in 2001, housing prices did not fall, despite steep job losses. If there is a more severe correction in prices in 2006, home ownership gains will depend on demographic demand—not a continuation of the current economic conditions.

OVERSPENDING FOR HOMES

The increased availability of low-barrier entry loans that are readily purchased by Fannie Mae and Freddie Mac may be impacting the number of people who are buying homes beyond their suggested price range. As referenced in Chapter 1, a *Wall Street Journal* Online/ Harris Interactive Personal Finance Poll found that nearly one in five (19 percent) U.S. adults who purchased homes within the last three years for their primary residences said they spent *above* their suggested price range, two-thirds (67 percent) stayed *within* their price range, and 12 percent were *below* their price range.

When obtaining mortgages for new homes, home buyers who used a mortgage broker, direct lender, or another source were nearly three times more likely to obtain a fixed-rate mortgage (72 percent) than an adjustable-rate mortgage (26 percent). Astonishingly, one-third (34 percent) opted for a creative or option mortgage.

Regional differences were obvious. With fewer than 17 percent of home buyers able to buy the median-priced home in California in 2005, it is not surprising to find that some West Coast home buyers (29 percent) were much more likely to have bought *beyond* their suggested price range. The more conservative Northeast (8 percent) and Midwest (12 percent) home buyers were less likely to incur such risk, but Southern home buyers, driven by gains in Florida and the Gulf Coasts of Mississippi and Alabama, were slightly less risk-averse (22 percent).

Thirty-nine percent of the online-respondents suggested they used mortgage brokers, while 32 percent used direct lenders, and 14 percent indicated they did not need a mortgage to purchase their homes. Younger home buyers (aged 18 to 34) were most likely to have chosen a broker (55 percent), while home buyers aged 35 to 42 were most likely to have obtained their mortgage through a direct lender (42 percent).

HIGH-RISK LOANS

As mentioned in Chapter 1, interest-only loans (IO), option-adjustable rate mortgages (O-ARMs), and piggyback loans are on the rise. A little more than one-third (34 percent) of the recent home buyers who obtained their mortgages through a broker, direct lender, or someone else chose one of the following four types of creative mortgages:

1. *Interest-only mortgage*—where borrowers pay interest but no principal for a fixed period at the beginning of the loan (17 percent)

2. *Piggyback mortgage*—where the loan combines a standard first mortgage with a home-equity loan or line of credit to avoid private mortgage insurance or the higher interest rates on jumbo loans (10 percent)

3. *Payment option mortgage*—where borrowers have four payment options each month, and those who elect to make the minimum payment could actually see their loan balance rise rather than fall (5 percent)

4. *Miss-a-payment mortgage*—where borrowers are allowed to skip up to 2 mortgage payments a year and up to 10 payments over the life of the loan without ruining their credit rating (2 percent)

So long as lenders do not require higher barriers to lend money, borrowers are likely to continue to buy their homes using other people's money, in anticipation of capital gains when they sell. Home buyers may not realize that monthly payments on some types of specialty mortgages can increase by as much as 50 percent or more when the introductory period ends.

EXPERT'S VIEW

"We are warning home buyers to approach these new mortgages carefully," said Mike Calhoun, general counsel of the Center for Responsible Lending. "They should be cautious about accepting a mortgage they can't afford. These kinds of mortgages can be devastating for families who are stretching their budget to buy a home."

In 2004, one in four loans was financed with an interest-only loan. Three years previously, interest-only loans were a mere fraction of the total loan products. On July 20, 2005, in testimony before the U.S. House of Representatives Committee on Financial Services, Alan

CURRENT MORTGAGE MARKET STRESS

	Percentage of Total	Comment
ARMs (January 2006)	31	Average
Interest-only (2005)	31 to 35	Moderately high
Percentage with LTV greater than 90% (January 2006)	16	Low

TABLE 4.1

Sources: Federal Housing Finance Board, LoanPerformance, Mortgage Bankers Association

Greenspan, then Federal Reserve Board chairman, expressed concern about the "increase in the prevalence of interest-only loans and the introduction of more exotic forms of adjustable-rate mortgages." He suggested that some home buyers may be using these kinds of loans to buy houses they might not otherwise afford. He warned that lenders should "fully appreciate the risk that some households may have in meeting monthly payments as interest rates and the macroeconomic climate change." (See Table 4.1.)

UNEMPLOYMENT

Stating the obvious, job income is most crucial to the health of the housing market. You may think that the house you buy is the collateral that banks use to give you a loan, but it is actually your job that the bank considers. Real estate values can rise and fall, and there are terrific penalties for skipping housing payments. Banks do not really want to be in the business of managing repossessed real estate; they just want borrowers to repay their loans. In areas with rapid rates of housing appreciation, a household that experiences a job loss or some other kind of economic shock can more easily sell its home in order to remove the mortgage liability. However, in weaker housing markets, homeowners may not be able to sell their homes as quickly. These borrowers are more likely to linger in delinquency, which could force a lender to proceed with foreclosure.

Just in time for the holidays, employers added 215,000 jobs in November 2005, up from 44,000 in October, keeping the unemployment rate at 5 percent. The November gains matched average job growth during the first part of the year, before it was blown off course by Hurricanes Katrina and Rita. Out of 278 industries, over 62 percent reported gains—the most positive record since May 2004.

What really had economists cheering was that the job gains were broad based. Construction added 37,000 jobs, professional services added 29,000, and manufacturing added 11,000. Retail added a holiday season (adjusted) 9,000 jobs. With average hourly earnings at $16.32, wages were also up over 3 percent for the year, but that was not enough to cover the 4.3 percent gain in prices ending in October, according to the Labor Department.

> This means inflation was gaining on
> America's payrolls and checkbooks.

By June 2006, interest rates were approaching 7 percent. Both the NAR and the National Association of Home Builders reported slowing volume in sales, dropping by as much as 5 to 20 percent in some of the most active metros. Yet prices didn't drop. While home prices appreciated 13 percent in 2005, appreciation had slowed to 7 percent by mid-year 2006.

Some economists wondered whether higher interest rates might cause some of those jobs in construction to go away if the housing market softens further in 2006, but new housing sales remain robust, although slower, in 2006.

The government states that it takes six months to establish a trend, and that one month's statistics, up or down, are not cause for concern. That is why the Bureau of Labor Statistics outlook from 2004 to 2014 remains positive. In addition, consumer spending accounts for more than 70 percent of the gross domestic product.

The labor force, those aged 16 or older who are actively seeking work, is projected to grow by 1 percent annually, with certain occupations doing better in growth than others. Among 10 occupational groups, professional and service-related occupations will provide 60 percent of total job growth between 2004 and 2014, while office, administrative support, framing, fishing, and forestry jobs will decline.

Mother Nature and the Reduction of Union Wages

Peter Miller, author of *The Common-Sense Mortgage*, believes there is plenty of evidence that many jobs are in peril. "State economies (like those destroyed by Hurricanes Katrina and Rita) will need to be restarted—most likely this will be done with massive rebuilding projects that will create a new property and income base. As the Gulf area repopulates, state treasuries will be refilled over time . . . assuming other massive storms do not hit the same areas."

There is a different disaster across the Rustbelt. It involves not nature, but the reality that global wage rates are beginning to impact U.S. incomes. General Motors, according to the *New York Times*, is now building a truck in China for local consumption. The "Wuling Sunshine" minivan is tiny by U.S. standards, but it gets 43 miles per gallon (MPG) and sells for roughly $5,000. One reason for the low price is the local wage rate: workers are paid $60 a month.

In the Rustbelt, U.S. workers at Delphi (the huge auto parts supplier that has some 215,000 employees worldwide) have been getting $27 per hour. Worse for workers in America, China is planning to export cars of its own to the United States. This could possibly repeat the sucker punch to the American car industry that Japan wielded in the 1960s—a punch from which the Big Three, Ford, Chrysler, and GM, have yet to recover fully. Delphi filed for a Chapter 11 bankruptcy on October 8, 2005, in the hopes of reducing worker wages to between $10 to $12 an hour.

If worker wages drop, what happens to local home values, mortgage payments, neighborhood businesses, and community tax revenues?

If Delphi can reduce wages on the factory floor, other companies will pursue similar policies. However, this company that lost $338 million in the second quarter of 2005 laid off 6,175 workers over a 15-month period, while increasing severance packages for top executives. "We have seen jobs going overseas before: *maquiladoras* were established just across the Mexican border, call centers were built in India and Ireland, and textile production was exported to Malaysia, Indonesia, and the Philippines," warns Miller. "The issue is radically different this time; instead of moving jobs overseas, lower wages are moving here."

THE BUBBLE NEWS STORIES

The news media is frothy with bubble stories. Using "housing bubble" as the search, Google returned over 10,500,000 results on July 21, 2006, many of which are news stories that hype a coming crash in real estate prices. One story even suggested the government needed to rein in the housing market by overturning the Taxpayer Relief Act of 1997. This Act allows homeowners to keep millions in capital gains, which the government could then apply to reduce the huge government deficit.

Yet the media fails to notice inconsistencies. In a February 2004 speech, Alan Greenspan, then Federal Reserve chairman, suggested that fixed-rate mortgages were expensive, and that home buyers should consider adjustable-rate mortgages to reduce housing costs. What made this advice so strange at the time was that fixed-rate mortgages were at near 30-year lows. The economy was poised to turn upward, which would take interest rates up with it, putting home buyers with adjustable-rate mortgages at more risk.

In his July 2005 testimony before Congress, Greenspan had apparently forgotten his earlier observation that fixed-rate mortgages are a tad expensive. "The apparent froth in housing markets appears to have interacted with evolving practices in mortgage markets," he said. "The increase in the prevalence of interest-only loans and the introduction of more exotic forms of adjustable-rate mortgages are developments of particular concern."

(By the time Ben Bernanke took over as chairman of the Fed in February 2006, inflation was the party pooper to watch. By July, the Fed had raised short-term interest rates no less than 17 times in 18 months, causing long-term interest rates [mortgage interest rates] to go up too. Many felt that if the Fed overcorrected, there would be a housing crash, yet if it didn't go far enough in controlling monetary policy, inflation would get out of hand and we'd see a return to the 1970s and early 1980s, when mortgage interest rates soared in the double digits.)

Should we really be surprised? These products of concern expand the yield spread between fixed-rate and adjustable-rate loans enough to make it worth the risk to ride out rising rates. If people can grab some real estate and make more money than they ever dreamed of in the stock market with less risk, is it any wonder housing has been on an eight-year streak? And why would consumers who are having home buying made so easy for them assume that they are making a mistake?

Instead, many believe that the real estate bubble will develop a slow leak, caused by rising interest rates and inflation concerns. Compared to the idea of a dramatic real estate downturn:

- The economy's still growing.
- Gas prices are rising, but families are absorbing the costs (despite record profits announced by Exxon for fourth-quarter 2005).
- Children of the Baby Boomers are buying their first homes.
- Property value appreciations are softening to a more normalized 3 to 5 percent pace for 2006.

But the financial press is pressing on. They want to see a crash with lots of blood.

The Impact of the Financial Press

Ashamed of its failure to report signs of weakness in the stock market before it took a knee-capping tumble in 2000, the financial press appears determined not to let the housing boom move forward without regular doses of pessimism. But some feel they have gone overboard. "After missing the tech and telecom bubbles, the generals of the financial media are now battling more bubbles than we can count," writes Barry Withholtz (www.Realmoney.com, May 2005). "There are bubbles in debt, credit, and interest rates. There is the oil bubble, the import bubble, the China bubble, and the current account deficit bubble. In short, we have a veritable bubble in bubbles. Indeed, it is astonishing how many people who failed to either acknowledge the tech bubble in the 1990s or at least failed to act on it now have no hesitation to declare real estate to be a bubble."

Is the financial press trying to "worry" the nation into shifting its money from real estate back into stocks?

Al Yoon, www.Bloomberg.com reporter, wrote in December 2005, "In the U.S. bond market, the housing bubble has burst. Bonds backed by home loans to the riskiest borrowers, the fastest growing part of the $7.6 trillion mortgage market, have lost about 2.5 percent since September. An 18-month rise in interest rates may force more than 150,000 consumers into default."

Christopher Farrell (*BusinessWeek*, August 2005) suggested that the government needs to rein in the housing market. He advocated overturning the Taxpayer Relief Act of 1997 that allows homeowners to skip paying taxes on capital gains derived from homestead sales.

The real danger is that constant talk about a housing bubble could single-handedly cause housing prices to moderate, slip, or slide. It can force buyers to wring their hands on the sidelines—wondering if they should jump into a game they are not certain they will win in the near future.

There are plenty of pundits out there who are trying to affect what Greenspan, Bernanke, and company did not accomplish early enough—a housing market that has absorbed one-third of the nation's investment wealth. That could account for the negative attention housing is receiving from the financial press.

Bubble stories have been in the press since 2002, faithfully recounting government incentives, a raging stock market, falling inflation and interest rates, a more restrained home-building industry, and low interest rates as contributors to moving housing upward. But they have also pointed out how housing prices have defied reason by going higher during a recession fueled by record low interest rates and flat employment. Housing prices have risen while stock prices plummeted. Homes have been a virtual ATM, with homeowners removing cash in equity loans and refinancing $350 billion in 2001 and 2002—spending $70 billion and holding $165 billion in checking and money market accounts. Housing's impact on the economy was unprecedented, allowing it to stretch instead of shrink.

Irresponsible Journalism In response to a *Fortune* story, Alex Perriello, president and CEO of Realogy Franchise Group (Coldwell Banker, ERA, CENTURY 21, Sotheby's) pointed out that the $1.2 million house that was featured as "overpriced" happened to be a Coldwell Banker listing, which in 1996 was on the verge of being condemned. The owner invested several hundred thousand dollars to improve it, putting it "on par with other properties in the San Francisco area."

EXPERT'S VIEW

"Since 1969, the first year the nation's average home sale prices were tracked by HUD, there has never been a year that the nation's average sales price has not risen," says Alex Perriello. Even through the oil crisis of 1978 through 1982, "while there was a 50 percent drop in the number of homes sold; prices still rose." National research indicates that the demographics exist to sustain the growth of the real estate market.

Does the financial press have it in for real estate?

"I have a drawer full of these stories," Perriello says. "Most every negative story I read about real estate is supported by anecdotal evidence and speculation. Quite frankly I'm getting sick and tired of irresponsible journalism that attacks one of the few bright spots in the U.S. economy . . . housing."

What about the Local Level What does the press have to gain by talking about a "housing bubble"? It knows it cannot make up for missing the tech bubble, but it does not seem to understand that it also cannot treat the housing market like the stock market. Typically, most bubble stories concentrate on overheated markets like Boston or San Francisco and relate their conclusions to the rest of the nation. There is no national market—housing recessions and booms take place at the local level.

With hundreds of thousands of articles written over the last few years about the real estate housing bubble, Wall Street may be attempting to influence journalists into accomplishing what market fundamentals have so far failed to do—*let the air out*. The hope is that investors, who have sidelined a seesawing stock market tarnished by mismanagement, lies, and fraud, will stop buying homes and start buying stocks again.

Is Wall Street really trying to undermine housing?

According to Thomas Prendergast, a funds professional, there seems to have been tension between the real estate industry and Wall Street because they sometimes compete for the same investment/spending dollars. However, that is no proof that journalists have a vested interest in steering money away from real estate and back toward Wall Street.

If housing were to collapse or even decline, the effects would not benefit Wall Street because much of the U.S. job market has been related to the housing industry, including construction, financing, and home furnishings. In addition, no one wants to see mortgages go into default, since businesses and consumers alike would suffer.

So, it may be the rabble-rousing press that is blowing hot air into bubble talk, not Wall Street. The fact of the matter is that Wall Street is largely positive or neutral regarding the outlook for real estate. It shares the NAR's view that the rate of price increases and market turnover will simply slow in an orderly fashion.

This was proven by mid-year 2006: housing had slowed, and the NAR predicted that by year-end existing home sales would drop 6.8 percent to 6.60 million from the record 7.08 million set in 2005. New homes sales would fall 13.4 percent from the record 1.28 million sales in 2005, and housing starts would decline 6.2 percent to 1.94 million compared to 2.07 million in 2005. That's scary, unless you know those figures are about equal to the records set in 2003.

Said David Lereah, NAR's chief economist, on January 6, 2006, "Now the housing market has cooled, but 2006 is still expected to be the third strongest on record. In this case, experiencing a slowing from a hot market is a good thing because we need a solid housing sector to provide an underlying base to the economy, and slower appreciation will help to preserve long-term affordability."

LACK OF AFFORDABILITY

In 2005, Harvard economists found that nearly one in three American households (the 28 million households in the bottom half of the economy) spent more than 30 percent of their income on housing; more than one in eight spent upwards of 50 percent. In addition, there is a clear divide between median home buyers and the average American. The NAR's 2005 Profile of Home Buyers and Sellers suggested that the median income of home-buying households was $71,600, while the median income of first-time home buyers was $57,200.

While most families with median incomes can afford the median-priced home in their areas, in some regions affordability is a problem. For example, during 2005, California reached a nadir—only 16 percent of households could afford the median-priced home, which by then was over $500,000, a new price record, according to the California Association of REALTORS®. In 2005, Northeast home buyers had a median income of at least $71,500, a decline of 1.2 percent over 2004, while Midwest home buyers had the lowest median income at $66,800. West Coast home buyers had the highest median income at $75,000, and the South was middling with $72,500 as the median income for home buyers in 2005.

Cost-Burdened Homeowners

Housing affordability for lower-income families has deteriorated over the past several years. According to the U.S. Census Bureau's most recent American Housing Survey, more than 70 percent of the families with incomes in the lowest quintile spent 30 percent or more of their income on housing. Forty-six percent of those families spent more than half of their income on a home mortgage or rental payments.

However, affordability is not a crisis for just the 28 million households in the bottom half of the income stream. It is also impacting middle-income households. From 2000 to 2003, the number of middle-income households with severe housing cost burdens shot up by nearly 1 million. In fact, the cost of owning exceeded the cost of renting by 30 percent nationally, making renting a bargain in some areas.

Escalating home prices have reached record numbers for the last five years, with house price appreciation outpacing per capita income gains by more than four times in 31 metros and three times in 32 metros. This has created a housing wealth effect for those already in the housing market. Out of 163 of the nation's largest metros, there is double-digit housing appreciation in 53 of them.

Not only do escalating home values set the bar higher for entry into home ownership, other costs such as property taxes and utilities rise too. Economists say that more than 37 percent of the central city households are cost-burdened, while 30 percent of the suburban households and 24 percent of the nonmetro households are cost-burdened. (See Figure 4.3.)

Distance from Work Long, gas-guzzling commutes to and from affordable housing, located far from work centers can add as much as 10 percent to household budgets. The number of large metros where more than half of the households live 10 miles or more from central

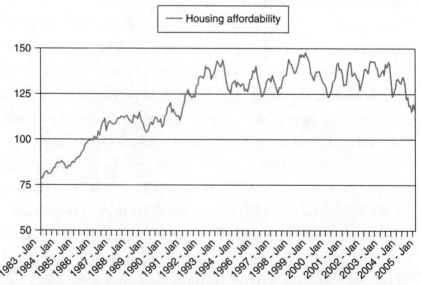

FIGURE 4.3 *Housing Affordability Tumbling to Lowest in Fifteen Years*
Source: National Association of REALTORS®

business districts (CBDs) has more than tripled since 1970. Many cities such as Austin, Kansas City, and Sacramento house one-fifth of their workers more than 20 miles from their urban centers. Several metropolitan statistical areas (MSAs) extend even further, say the economists, with one-third of Boston's households and one-quarter of San Francisco's households living 30 miles from the CBD.

Disparity among Racial Groups According to the report, another cause for concern is the disparity in home ownership among racial groups. Minority respondents were evenly divided on the question of whether high costs forced them to rent rather than buy, while just 28 percent of whites reported high housing costs as the reason they rent. In addition, nearly 45 percent of the minorities reported commutes of an hour or more, compared to only 28 percent among whites. In addition, occupants struggle to hold down housing costs by living in crowded conditions and poorly repaired and maintained structures.

Rising Interest Rates Rising interest rates, while still extremely affordable historically, are beginning to crowd home buyers. In addition to having to come up with more for the down payment on a home that costs 15 percent more than last year, buyers are paying about $100 more per month in new loans acquired at the end of 2005 than they did in 2003.

EXPERT'S VIEW

"The high cost of housing is placing enormous stress on families, affecting every aspect of their lives," said Rick Davis, president of the Homeownership Alliance. "Whether it is education, work-life balance, or more general quality of life issues, the poll shows that families are feeling the pressure of high housing costs."

FORECLOSURES

Until 1973, there were only three ways to finance a home in the United States: Federal Housing Authority (FHA), Veteran's Administration (VA), and conventional loan. That is the year the private mortgage insurance entered the market, allowing lenders to take more risk and opening up home loans to more people in order to qualify them to buy homes. The sad fact is that some home loans go bad and result in foreclosure, the legal action a lender can use to take back part or all of the property to satisfy the debt.

Foreclosure is an ugly, painful process that neither lenders nor borrowers take lightly. It generally begins shortly after the borrower misses a payment for principal, interest, taxes, or insurance, and the lender declares a default. The acceleration of the mortgage debt varies according to the type of loan, state law, and the policies of the lender. Default can also be triggered by failure to maintain a property, but is less common than nonpayment of installments. Unlike bankruptcy that is a federal debt-relief program, the foreclosure process is governed by the real estate/property laws of the state where the property is located.

The Mortgage Bankers Association of America (MBAA) did a quarterly study of about 40 million active mortgage loans and determined that by mid-year 2005, approximately 4.3 percent of the loans were in default, and about 1 percent of the loans were in foreclosure.

A monthly foreclosure report done by RealtyTrac, an online real estate portal specializing in foreclosures, determined that by December 2005, foreclosures had increased 25 percent for the total year—one new foreclosure for every 1,422 U.S. households. That is still relatively low; however, what is worrisome is that the effects of exotic loans on a declining housing market have yet to be tested.

Reasons for Default

There are many reasons that loans go into default, including loss of income, family loss, serious illness, divorce, and mortgage fraud. The MBAA's latest 2005 study found that foreclosures are not necessarily highest where you think they might be: in California. In fact, California, where median home prices rose by another 25.2 percent, had a late-payment rate of only 1.88 percent.

According to Washington, D.C., real estate columnist Ken Harney, "The highest rates of late payments and foreclosures are in states that have relatively slow-rising home prices, slow-growing economies, and above-average unemployment." While it may seem counterintuitive, foreclosures tend to be highest in those areas where there have been factory layoffs and high unemployment. Though the national average rate of foreclosure was 1 percent as of mid-year, Ohio homeowners had a 3.3 percent rate, followed by Indiana at 2.8 percent, Kentucky with 1.9 percent, and Mississippi at 1.7 percent. The lowest rates (all under 0.5 percent) in the United States, by contrast, were in some of the highest-fizz markets: California, Hawaii, Virginia, Arizona, New Hampshire, and Vermont.

Many homeowners in trouble do not realize there are alternatives to foreclosure. Nearly two-thirds of borrowers behind on their payments are unaware of the workout options available to them, according to a December 2005 study by Freddie Mac. It is hard to imagine that foreclosures could be even higher were it not for lenders with "loss mitigation" programs "that allow delinquent borrowers to stay in their houses and work out their problems," suggests Harney. Some basic restructuring techniques include deferring arrearages to the final payoff of the loan; decreases in note rates; and sales-in-lieu of foreclosure, which allow seriously delinquent borrowers to sell their properties to pay off the loan balance prior to foreclosure.

MORTGAGE FRAUD

Michigan real estate broker Ralph Roberts says one in four mortgage loan transactions is fraudulent. He should know—he is working with the FBI to slow down the massive numbers of fraudulent transactions that are threatening the health of the real estate market. "This is the biggest lending crisis since the savings and loan meltdown of the late 1980s," he says.

Most of the fraud schemes involve variations of several of the following elements in which the "fraudsters":

- Pay "straw borrowers" or "investors" to sign and submit documents containing false qualifying information (such as false and counterfeit drivers' licenses, pay stubs, tax returns, etc.)
- Induce appraisers to inflate property values in order to obtain a larger mortgage loan for the "straw borrower"
- Submit bogus invoices for phantom "upgrades" or "renovations" that falsely inflate the value of the property (allowing the fraudster to obtain a larger mortgage)
- Promise "investors" that their properties will be leased or rented and all mortgage, insurance, property tax, and homeowner association payments will be paid for them, while these payments are *not* made and there may or may not be any tenants
- Pay "straw sellers" to falsely claim ownership of a property, appear at a closing where the property is sold to "straw borrowers," disburse the sale proceeds at the fraudsters' direction, and thereafter appear at another closing to purchase the same property at a lesser amount with a portion of the sale proceeds

According to Roberts, "The scheme, commonly called 'house flipping,' has become a problem across the United States, especially in low-income neighborhoods." *Flipping* (buying a house and then quickly reselling it for a big profit) becomes a federal crime when it is part of a scam to defraud banks into approving mortgage loans for more than the property is worth, typically as a result of the submission of false appraisals and loan documents.

The National Consumer Law Center recently reported that the growth in the cottage industry of "foreclosure rescuers" has been triggered by a booming real estate market of fast-appreciation home prices. Higher home prices lead some homeowners to creative financing deals, but later, as interest rates rise, in the case of adjustable-rate mortgages (ARMs), the loans become too expensive. Likewise, appreciating home values give more and more owners equity to tap as cash for expenditures they may not have otherwise considered. This in turn can lead to payments they cannot afford.

DEBT ADDICTION

Salaries and wages are going up, according to a new report by the Bureau of Economic Analysis. And right now the outlook is positive. Personal income increased by nearly $53 billion or half a percent in June 2005, along with equally strong growth in personal disposable income.

However, Americans seem to see no reason to save money. Personal savings fell to zero percent in June—the second lowest savings rate since the Great Depression nearly 75 years ago. Since 1999, homeowners have watched their home values grow by more than two-thirds, giving the average household a net worth of $400,000.

In fact, Americans cannot spend their money fast enough. Although some mortgage activity has slowed due to a slight rise in interest rates, homeowners are refinancing and are still taking cash out of their

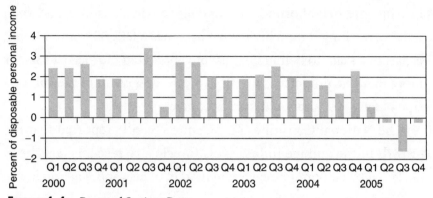

FIGURE 4.4 *Personal Savings Rates*
Source: U.S. Department of Commerce, Bureau of Economic Analysis

homes. Three-quarters of the homeowners refinancing a $100,000 loan increased their loan amount to $105,000. Once upon a time, homeowners refinanced to take advantage of lower interest rates. Not so today. They refinance to improve cash flow or to buy big ticket items. (See Figure 4.4.)

Luckily for the housing industry, Americans are putting a lot of their money into homes. According to Harvard's Joint Center for Housing Studies, Americans paid $133 billion for home improvements in the 12 months ending June 30, 2005. However, others were tempted by GM's and Ford's "employee" or "family" deals that enabled car buyers to buy cars at the discounts that employees pay. Homeowners also used their equity to buy second homes and to pay off credit card debt.

If consumers do not get control of their debts, from credit cards to equity loans, things could tumble for the economy. Lenders will have no choice but to rein in loans. For that reason, Lending Tree has performed a multiyear study called "Living with Debt: A Life Stage Analysis of Changing Attitudes and Behaviors." The report found that the social stigma of debt, which would have mortified previous generations, is largely lacking in our younger generations. They accumulate debt early in life and tend to want to experience immediate gratification rather than having traditional values like "saving for a rainy day."

Dividing participants into college students, young singles, young families, mature families, empty nesters, and seniors, the study found the following:

- With little training or preparation for personal finance, college students are not aware of the long-term consequences of their reliance on credit. (They view consumer credit as a reward for their hard work at school.)
- Graduating to first jobs with a burden of debt that they believe they can manage with high salaries, young singles are driven by competitive consumption and soaring home prices to spend more of their allotted income on housing than previous generations. (They believe they will be able to cash in on home equity gains.)
- Young families are more likely to use credit and accumulate debt as they compete with one another to outfit and to educate their children.
- Mature families are led by parents with restraint for themselves, but none where their children are concerned. (They lavish teenagers with what they believe is the socially expected level of material abundance, underfunding their retirement and raising their debt picture in the process.)
- Empty nesters are preparing for retirement, but admit they have not succeeded in transmitting their "traditional values of thrift and self-discipline to their children."
- Only seniors, shaped by the economic scarcities of the Great Depression and World War II, are able to use credit prudently, sometimes to their own disadvantage.

ADDITIONAL RISKS

What is happening is scary enough, but what might happen is even scarier. Lee Howlet, president and COO of Fiserv Lending Solutions—Fulfillment Services Division, says there are other risk factors to be aware of.

Regulators Might Become More Restrictive

Look for the FDIC to become more diligent in its overseeing of home equity lending and flexible-payment first-mortgage practices. We saw the beginnings of this more restrictive approach in the guidelines lenders received last year. In those guidelines, regulators expressed concern that some lenders were not being as diligent as they should be in monitoring the origination risk and performance of their loan portfolios. We expect to see an increased use of automated property valuation to help mitigate the overall risks with home equity loans, plus a greater use of value insurance products to help lenders offset the risks associated with alternative products.

Secondary Markets Will Demand More Due Diligence from Lenders

Expect lenders to increase the scrutiny of their portfolios with an eye to the concerns of Wall Street. The secondary market will be looking for lenders to do more thorough due diligence on their portfolio of loans with respect to the values and underwriting practices. Because of the perceived real estate bubble, we believe the secondary market will demand increased "auditing" of values. They will be attempting to identify risks within their portfolios aggressively, provide solutions to help mitigate those risks, and more quickly eliminate problem loans.

What If Consumers Stop Spending?

With a national savings rate below zero, consumers are already dipping into savings and taking out personal loans to make purchases. Every home bought and sold is associated with a certain amount of subsequent economic activity. Home buyers spend money on new furniture, remodeling, appliances, landscaping, and decorating. Each home purchase is also associated with services. As volume in both home buying and refinancing declines, real estate agents, appraisers, movers, title companies, and mortgage brokers will be competing for fewer customers. It makes sense to expect that as sales volume declines, so will economic activity.

National Bubbles versus Metro Bubbles

While most economists agree that there is no such thing as a national bubble, there are certainly influences that can impact housing markets at the local level: catastrophic news, the overall economy, and mortgage interest rates, to name a few. All have lenders and others watching the markets closely for potential risk.

THE PMI QUARTERLY RISK INDEX

As one of the lenders assisting in getting more people into homes, PMI Mortgage Insurance Co. (a subsidiary of The PMI Group, Inc.) releases a quarterly Risk Index. The Risk Index is not based on what you may think it is: that too many people are getting loans with private mortgage insurance. In contrast, the risk factors are actually broad market indicators such as employment and the economy as a whole.

EXPERT'S VIEW

"It's not about loans. It's not about risk in our business (under-writing and insuring loans). It is about home price appreciation and depreciation," explained Josh Wozman from The PMI Group, Inc. "This speaks to a number of factors in Metropolitan Statistical Areas (MSAs), like employment data, home price appreciation, etc. The Group then uses this data to determine which MSAs are more risky to insure loans."

Housing Prices Decline

Since autumn 2004, PMI's Risk Index data showed that the average risk value of the 50 largest MSAs was 186, implying an 18.6 percent probability of an overall house price decline.

In January 2005, based on PMI's Risk Index model, the average risk value of the 50 largest MSAs was 161, which means there is a 16.1 percent probability of an overall house price decline within the next two years. During winter 2005, average risk value decreased sequentially, quarter-over-quarter, to 134 or a 13.4 percent risk.

In March 2005, the report indicated a decrease in the probability of an overall house price decline, except for the riskiest MSAs—nine of which were on the east and west coasts. In other words, California had a higher likelihood of home depreciation than other areas.

Analysts at PMI attributed the average decrease in risk to improving nationwide economic conditions indicated by generally lower regional unemployment rates and increasing (or less negative) job creation. Even so, eight of the nine MSAs ranked at the top of PMI's Risk Index did experience a substantial increase in risk.

By January 2006, the risk index rose. Thirty-two of the nation's 50 largest housing markets were at an increased risk of price declines—

a 25 percent increase in risk of price declines. The new index at 168 suggested a 16.8 percent risk of declines.

PMI identified 11 markets with a greater than 50 percent chance of experiencing price declines, up from 5 markets the previous quarter. In the 50 percent bracket, San Diego, CA, now tops the list with a 58.8 percent chance of price declines, followed by Santa Ana, CA; Boston, MA; Long Island (Nassau-Suffolk), NY; Oakland, CA; Sacramento, CA; Riverside, CA; Providence, RI; Los Angeles, CA; San Jose, CA; and San Francisco, CA.

By summer 2006, the Risk Index had skyrocketed to 288, with 50 of the nation's largest housing markets at risk of a 28.8 percent decline in prices.

PMI expects slowing to continue as appreciation in many markets is still in the double-digits—high by historical standards (a rate of 4 to 6 percent annually is considered normal in the United States). A continued gradual slowing of appreciation will contribute to a soft landing, provided that the U.S. and regional economies remain robust (unharmed by economic shocks, unforeseen events, or an adverse change in consumer sentiment), suggests Mark Milner, chief risk officer of PMI Mortgage.

EXPERT'S VIEW

"In this more normal environment of slower appreciation and higher interest rates, it's a good time for consumers to consider the risks they can control, namely the type of mortgage they have. It may pay to limit interest rate and payment shock risk by locking in a fixed rate or a substantial fixed-rate period on a fully amortizing loan. If the borrower has limited funds for a down payment, mortgage insurance should be considered," says Mark Milner.

According to PMI, the five least risky areas are Nashville, TN; Cincinnati, OH; Indianapolis, IN; Memphis, TN; and Pittsburgh, PA.

VALUATION INDEX

By October 2005, PMI was enjoying the popularity of its Risk Index and decided to issue a Valuation Index. This new index tracks home price appreciation patterns over several decades for major MSAs and evaluates current deviations from the historical norms. This makes it seem suspiciously like the Risk Index (*without the risk*).

While this report followed the loss of millions of homes due to Hurricanes Katrina and Rita in August, it found that the most overvalued properties in October were located in California, specifically, Los Angeles (33.7 percent), San Jose (26.5 percent), and San Diego (22.3 percent). "Las Vegas is 25.5 percent overvalued and Phoenix-Scottsdale is 22 percent," wrote Ken Harney for Realty Times. On the East Coast, the most overvalued markets were northern New Jersey (25.6 percent), New York's Long Island (20.4 percent), Providence (19.1 percent), Miami (20.5 percent), Tampa-St. Petersburg (23.2 percent), Orlando (19.6 percent), and Washington, D.C. (18.2 percent).

Bargain hunters can have fun shopping for homes in undervalued Denver, where the index puts property values at 4.2 percent below where they should be, Detroit (−10.3 percent), Charlotte (−1 percent), Cleveland (−1.4 percent), and Memphis (−1.7 percent). Other markets the Valuation Index concludes are relatively safe bets—at or just slightly above where they should be—include Pittsburgh, Kansas City, Minneapolis, Atlanta, and Ft. Worth. Austin and San Antonio are other seemingly safe bets in Texas, but Dallas prices are a little riskier—10.5 percent above where they should be, according to PMI.

Despite the ravaging storms of the season, the economy actually expanded in September 2005, according to the Beige Book (a report compiled by the Federal Reserve). Areas such as Dallas and Atlanta were disrupted. Even though they were not in the paths of the storms, they took in thousands of storm refugees and provided millions of dollars in services to them. Along with Richmond and Philadelphia, Dallas and Atlanta passed on higher prices to consumers, but the Beige Book noted that firms in San Francisco, Chicago, and Boston did not have pricing power or the ability to pass on higher prices.

Housing markets remained strong or were growing in the San Francisco and St. Louis regions. Weakness in sales or construction was noted in parts of the Richmond district as well as in the Boston, Chicago, Cleveland, Kansas City, and New York districts.

Of course, when speculators play an area out, they move on, causing a "rolling boom." They move their investment fever to a new area, making cities like Dallas and Atlanta attractive targets for speculation while, in effect, helping to create a new bubble.

There is plenty of housing available at affordable prices in both cities. Dallas and Atlanta are both overdue for market corrections and undervalued by PMI standards. Like other areas that suffered from the dot-com meltdown, both lost their share of high-paying jobs and have struggled to attract opportunities back to their business centers.

Even with solid data,
you can still be wrong about whether
a market is at risk of a bust.

BOOMS DON'T LAST FOREVER

Between 1978 and 2003, the nationwide home price index (HPI) grew an average of 5 percent per year in nominal terms, barely beating inflation at about 3.5 percent. Yet in some communities, housing appreciation reached 20 to 25 percent—a pace that is not sustainable over the long term. So, is it likely that a bust will occur? Not necessarily. If it takes a severe economic shock to cause a population to move away (which is what precipitates a bust), then it stands to reason that it is population demand that moves home prices either higher or lower.

How does that relate to recent housing price gains? Well, it is hard to look back at historical data and come to meaningful conclusions because there are conditions present today that were not present even 10 years ago. This is largely a result of many people buying homes, not because of jobs, but because of return on investment.

This type of boom is driven by tremendous tax incentives and easy credit. There is not a similar period in recent economic history that we can use for comparison. This is one reason I feel that the Taxpayer Relief Act and easy credit are strong reasons for the recent housing boom of the last eight years, which resulted in 33 boom markets by 2003. The next greatest boom period was in 1988, with 24 boom markets. That is why this boom is different—it's more widespread, leading onlookers to assume that it's a nationwide phenomenon.

BUT BOOMS DON'T ALWAYS END IN BUSTS

That's what makes it something of a puzzle that so many people are worried about a *national* housing bubble. While house values can certainly recede, it is not as if homeowners do not have continued use of their homes. You may want to set fire to it, but you still own something. That something could very well recover and exceed its current value, barring some unforeseen catastrophic event.

However, consider the stock market. Nextgreatidea.com can go public with a graduate student CEO, who learns that his or her next great idea had better materialize every quarter or those demanding shareholders will punish the stock and its management. And should the worst happen—*gasp,* bankruptcy—it is usually only the shareholders who are left holding the bag, because management has long since bailed out with a golden parachute.

Unlike worthless shares, when values recede
on a house you still have the house.

Home price declines are relatively rare. They generally accompany severe and prolonged job losses, such as the auto industry meltdown that impacted Michigan and Ohio so negatively in the 1980s. In fact, home prices have not declined, according to the NAR, since the Great Depression of the 1930s. Home prices have held up against stock market collapses, the OPEC oil crisis, economic recessions, war, and terrorist attacks on American soil.

One reason homes do not suffer losses like other financial assets is that they are not traded very often. Homeowners trade homes once every 7 to 10 years, at a cost of approximately 10 to 14 percent of the sale price, including commissions and other closing costs on both sides of the transaction. That is quite a premium to pay to change homes, not including moving costs.

If a homeowner is in a must-sell position, it is usually because of a family or job change. People do not tend to sell their homes in a panic to lock in gains or avoid losses. This is because losses, even in the worst of times, do not tend to be nearly as precipitous as losses in other financial assets.

CHAPTER
5

THE BUST TO COME

Is the Federal Government Trying to Slow Down Housing?

The U.S. Census Bureau has reported that the housing industry now represents over 25 percent of the U.S. investment dollars, with a 5 percent value in the overall economy, as well as over 15 percent of the gross domestic product. That should be a good thing, but not for those who are worried that housing is too hot and needs to be slowed down. The conundrum here is that while it is not the federal government's job to control asset prices, it does have a role in balancing the economy should it fall off the tightrope.

Back in July 2005, Alan Greenspan began to introduce fear into the housing market. He told Congress that there was some "froth" in some local markets. At the Federal Open Market Committee meeting, he suggested that housing prices were "unsustainable," and that the Fed would not use interest rates to address "possible misspricing."

In his famously stilted, inscrutable manner, Greenspan said that the lowered risk premiums coupled with greater productivity growth had propelled asset prices higher, including *homes*. When these assets were converted to cash, they became a "source of purchasing power." Easy refinance money reduced the cost of cash conversions.

However, an increase in the market value of asset claims is in part the indirect result of investors' accepting lower compensation for risk. In other words, if you buy at the top of the market, you will not be able to convert your asset into as much cash as easily.

Gold rushes (whether the asset class is tulips, Texas Instruments, or town homes) do not last long because increases in market value are too often viewed as never ending. Liquidity can freeze overnight; even the hint of elevated risk can lower asset values.

Translation: the economy might suddenly smack quick-buck investors who are highly leveraged in real estate.

By July 2006, the federal government had raised short-term interest rates no less than 17 straight times. Mortgage interest rates (30-year benchmark fixed rate) rose to nearly 7 percent, which is still low by historical standards, but the rise was enough to cause one of the steepest anticipated declines in housing appreciation ever, according to Walt Molony, senior associate with the NAR's research team. Housing went from 12.5 percent annual appreciation to under 8 percent by mid-year 2006, yet housing still beat inflation handily picking up speed at around 3 percent.

While short-term rates are not tied to long-term rates, they do have an impact on long-term lending rates, such as mortgage interest rates, that could be impacted by inflation. In an inflationary environment, lenders will raise interest rates to offset higher monetary costs down the road. But sometimes, mortgage interest rates do not always cooperate, keeping the risk premium attractive for home buyers who used low mortgage interest rates and low-entry loans to get into increasingly higher-priced homes.

Not everyone agreed that Greenspan and his successor Ben Bernanke were doing the economy any favors by kneecapping the housing industry's gains. Dr. Mark Skousen, chairman of *Investment U*, an investment e-letter, and adjunct faculty member of Columbia University, called Greenspan a "threat." Many economists are wary of the government's interference, believing that Greenspan and company took short-term interest rates too low by 2003 and may have overcorrected by increasing them too many times by 2006. Lenders want to loan money at higher rates than they pay for money. If the yield spread between long- and short-term rates is not broad enough, there are no incentives to loan long-term money.

In fact, by January 2006, the *yield spread* inverted several times, meaning that for a brief time, short-term money actually cost *more* than long-term money.

EXPERT'S VIEW

"The lesson from history is: whenever short-term interest rates rise above long-term interest rates, the economy goes into recession. In fact, for the last 40 years, whenever short-term rates rose above long-term rates, the economy dipped into recession," said Dr. Mark Skousen.

Things leveled out in mid-year 2006, but not before housing slowed considerably.

In 1990 and in 2000, short-term rates just briefly crossed below zero, triggering a recession. Needless to say, recessions have a huge impact on real estate and new-home prices. After a big rise in home prices in recent years, a fall in home prices in inflation-adjusted terms seems pretty certain, making a double-digit percentage fall possible. Recessions can follow booms; but, so do economic plateaus. New-home prices may adjust in a riskier environment, but they cannot be maintained without significant incentives to buyers during a recession.

In anyone's book, what is needed is a return to normal: where the median family can afford a median home. But do not count on wages to increase to allow households to buy homes. In January 2006, the Labor Department announced that employee compensation was up 3.1 percent in 2005. Although that was a smaller increase than in 2004 and the slowest rise since 2001, productivity was only up 2.7 percent. Unemployment also fell to a five-year low of 4.7 percent in January.

A decrease in unemployment should be good news, but the seesawing stock market responded by shedding over 150 points on the Dow Jones Industrial Average in two days, before sheepishly rising again. Inflation-watchers were clearly worried that wage prices, coupled with slower output, could spell trouble for the economy. However, there is a glass-half-full point of view: there are more people able to buy goods and services.

With existing home prices rising over 12 percent in 2005, from nearly 16 percent in 2004, housing is a natural scapegoat for the lack of momentum in the stock market. Quoting economist Christopher Farrell from a column for *BusinessWeek*, in sharp contrast to housing, "[C]apital gains on stocks and bonds carry a 15 percent levy [the capital gains tax rate had been 20 percent until the tax law change of 2003]. The powerful lure of tax-free profit is one reason that home prices have risen at a nearly 7 percent annual rate versus about 4 percent for the stock market since 1997. Sell a home with a $500,000 profit and owe Uncle Sam nothing. But realize that $500,000 gain on Nextbreakthroughtechnology.com and the federal government takes 15 percent. That's the kind of math most people can figure out."

Can't real estate and stocks both rise above
the rate of inflation—in harmony?

Homes and stocks cannot be compared like apples to apples. Homes are more than a calculated investment—they are a place to live, retreat, and regroup. Could that be the real reason buyers are willing to put more into housing? Is it possible that despite numbers to the contrary (one-third of homes were purchased by nonoccupying owners in 2004 and 2005), people buy homes because they want to?

"In the past, it seems that there have been tensions between the real estate industry and Wall Street as they sometimes compete for investment/spending dollars," acknowledges Thomas Prendergast, a managed funds professional, "steering money away from real estate and back toward Wall Street. This is no longer entirely accurate and may oversimplify the matter."

Wall Streeters are well aware of the wealth effect from house price appreciation—and that it exceeds the wealth effect of the stock market gains. However, a slower real estate market could have broad negative economic implications and would not benefit Wall Street. There are too many jobs related to housing—construction, financing, home furnishings, design, sales. No one in their right mind would want to threaten the underlying collateral on mortgages—jobs.

Yet, policy makers worry about the housing boom because of the disproportionate interest home buyers have in investing in housing due to tax incentives. This has fueled speculation in housing, which policy makers predict will inevitably end in a bust. But the housing market has one irrevocable advantage over stocks—if it loses value, property can still function as homes. Property does not implode, explode, melt down, burn up, or disappear—like evaporating stocks.

RISING INTEREST RATES

The National Association of REALTORS® (NAR) anticipates a near-record year in real estate sales for 2006, following five years of record-breaking sales. Rising interest rates may have an effect, but are higher rates really so bad?

Mortgage banker, author, and humorist David Reed is steamed about so-called experts trying to scare people by making them think rising interest rates are going to keep them from buying homes, or put them out of the homes they are in. During a radio interview with a Los Angeles station, Reed was paired with another guest, a financial planner.

The host of the show asked what rising rates would do to the housing market. The financial planner explained that rising rates meant homeowners would pay more money. On a $500,000 loan (typical for California) an extra 0.5 percent meant another $160 more each month in payments. Over the life of a 30-year loan, that meant another $57,000.

This would be a reason to worry, especially if homes do not increase in value for the next 30 years. However, the nearly 100 years of 3 percent average increase says this is unlikely. Plus, the borrower would have to keep the home for the life of the loan, which is extremely unlikely in the "day-trading twenty-first century." And does the financial planner think interest rates are going to improve any time soon?

Reed responded that rates have gone up, but gone up from what? "From record lows, that's what. Let's not get too spoiled here. Thirty-year fixed rates used to be in the high sevens and low eights way, way back in what? September 2000? Give me a break! Just take any historical mortgage rate chart and you will see that compared to rates going all the way back to the Paleolithic period, we are still in pretty good shape."

But this kind of "you say *tomato* and I say *tomahto*" is a typical argument between pundits. Reed believes it is irresponsible to tell people how "screwed they will be if they buy a house right now." Why? Because we cannot see into the future to make the necessary comparison. Sure, a half-point rise knocks some people out of home ownership, but there are other solutions—like buying a smaller house. "Instead of a $300,000 loan, get a $285,000 one," says Reed. "That's the typical qualifying difference between 6 percent and 6.5 percent."

The same goes for investors. Do not worry that interest rates are killing that market as well—it just means investors will have to buy smaller, less expensive homes. And quit worrying that there will be fewer homes sold in 2006. So what if sales equal 2005, 2004, or 2003? Each was a record-breaking year for both new and existing home sales.

"There is also the very real danger that consumers will misinterpret what they hear from pundits. Fair debate and honest discussions are one thing. Scaring consumers is quite another," says Reed. Yet, a slowing housing market is inevitable, especially with the *bubbleistas* out in force predicting that "the piper is about to be paid."

"In the past few years, nearly a third of all mortgage loans have been in the form of adjustable-rate mortgages (ARMs)," blared CNN in November 2005. And they are about to adjust, which means those who borrowed hybrid versions of ARMs are about to see their low-fixed-rate period end. The loan will reset to an adjustable rate that can fluctuate for the term of the loan.

The Mortgage Bankers Association estimates that some $330 billion worth of ARMs will adjust in 2006, and $1 trillion worth will reset by the end of 2007. This could have an impact, because more than 3 million homeowners (the average ARM loan is about $300,000) will pay larger mortgage payments for the duration of their loans' terms.

EXAMPLE

"If you took out a 3/1 ARM for $300,000 back in late 2002, your initial interest rate was probably around 5 percent and your monthly payment about $1,610," supposes CNN journalist, Les Christie. "The new payment, at a rate of about 7.1 percent, will adjust more than 2 percentage points to $1,995 per month, a difference of more than $385 monthly, or $4,600 annually."

That's a lot of money. If those ARMs reset in 2006 and 2007, the homeowners have the option to refinance into a fixed rate—providing they have enough equity in the home and can qualify for the new rate. "A 30-year fixed rate at 6.43 percent will still add about $260 a month to the borrower who had a 3/1 ARM. And the borrower will either have to pay about $3,000 to $5,000 in closing costs out-of-pocket or add that sum to the mortgage principal, sending monthly bills higher," warns Christie.

This can be a good thing for lenders. If ARMs adjust to a fully indexed 7.25 percent, loan officers will be refinancing them to another 5/1 ARM plan. Good loan officers will keep records of all their loan types and will later run a query on people who have adjustable or hybrids that are soon due for a reset. That can translate to about $1.3 trillion in new business.

LOSS OF HOMEOWNER TAX BENEFITS

What lawmakers were considering doing with current tax benefits could cost you thousands of dollars—annually. On September 2, 2004, President George Bush issued a press statement about his willingness to lead tax reform as a key priority. "Taxes should be applied fairly, and reform should recognize the importance of home ownership . . . in our American society," he said. He wrote an executive order in January 2005 to create an Advisory Panel to submit a report to the Secretary of the Treasury. The panel, composed of "experts, economists, and economically knowledgeable and experienced people of both political parties," was mandated to "fundamentally reform the tax code to make it simpler, fairer, and pro-growth."

Alarm bells started to ring early on for the housing and lending industries as the panel quickly homed in (pardon the pun) on homeowner tax benefits. The *Los Angeles Times* and others reported that the panel "tentatively agreed to recommend a substantial reduction in the limit on mortgage interest that homeowners could deduct from their taxes." Californians immediately became concerned as the median home price in the state—where one out of nine Americans live—was already well over $500,000. A cap on mortgage interest rate deduction could lead to an elimination of the benefit for all homeowners.

The panel looked at home ownership and health care as it sought to recommend the elimination of the Alternative Minimum Tax created in 1969 (that disallows many deductions to wealthy taxpayers). As inflation has risen with the years, the tax is impacting more and more middle-class taxpayers, as well as the wealthy. The panel estimates that the elimination of the Alternative Minimum Tax could cost the federal government approximately $1.2 trillion in revenue over a 10-year period. Those revenues would have to be made up. Yet, the panel offered "no estimate of the revenue to be gained by scaling back the mortgage deduction."

The problem with this kind of thinking is that no modeling has been done by any branch of the government. In other words, no one—including Bush—knows what the economic fallout would be if any current tax benefits were changed. They could only guess.

"They talked to lots of people," says Doug Duncan, chief economist for the Mortgage Bankers Association, who offered comments on what they thought would happen. "But here it is very simply—if you eliminate the [mortgage] deduction and property tax deductions, house prices will fall." A possible loss of tax benefits such as mortgage interest deductions (MIDs) would hurt taxpayers, as nearly 70 percent of Americans own homes. According to the NAR, not only would it effectively raise taxes on the middle class, but, in addition, the typical homeowner could lose $20,000 to $30,000 in housing equity.

The arguments are compelling on both sides. According to the Economics Department at MIT, the top 2.2 percent of tax returns claim 22 percent of the benefits from the mortgage interest rate deduction. However, the NAR volleys back that 52 percent of the families who claim the MID are the already beleaguered middle class—with incomes between $60,000 and $200,000.

One idea the panel put forward was replacing the mortgage interest rate deduction with a tax credit so all homeowners would benefit. Another was reducing the size of the mortgage upon which deductions could be taken. Currently, all mortgage interest is tax-deductible, allowing homeowners to take thousands off their income tax. If the MID is eliminated, it is proposed to be offset by a flat tax or sales tax, but the homeowner protest might prove to be too great. Home ownership is driven by the idea of owning, but that does not mean homeowners will want to see a major economic benefit reshuffled into a benefit that is opaque.

Mortgage Interest Tax Reform May Succeed

According to a joint study by the Housing and Urban Development and U.S. Census Bureau, nearly 40 percent of all residential properties in the United States, both owner-occupied and rental units, are owned free and clear with no mortgage. Further, 60 percent of all current mortgages originated four years prior to the 2001 survey. This eliminates a large number of homeowners who would protest mortgage interest tax deduction reform and gives credence to those who say the mortgage interest rate deduction is irrelevant to most homeowners. However, between 1991 and 2001, the total outstanding mortgage debt increased by more than 80 percent. It has continued to grow—increasing another 50 percent between 2001 and 2005.

Let's say the mortgage interest on a $150,000 loan at 6 percent is a little less than $9,000, plus property tax deductions, and any deductions for dependents. For married couples filing joint income taxes for 2005, the standard deduction was $10,000. For a head of household, the standard deduction for 2005 was $7,300, but the head of household would also likely add dependent deduction(s) to that amount. Singles have a standard $5,000 deduction and will be the most likely to benefit if their income is high enough to warrant itemizing, suggests California real estate educator Martha R. Williams, JD.

The tax reform panel has said it will be careful to suggest that changes be phased-in and that current homeowners be "grandfathered" so as to avoid upsetting the current housing market or harming current homeowners. However, that is not enough to soothe some real estate industry experts' fears.

EXPERT'S VIEW

"Housing is the engine that drives [the U.S.] economy . . . to even mention reducing the tax benefits of home ownership could endanger property values," warned Al Mansell, NAR's 2005 president. "The tax deductibility of interest paid on mortgages is both a powerful incentive for home ownership and one of the simplest provisions in the tax code. It should not be targeted for change."

The Tax Reform Act of 1986 proved that when tax benefits associated with real estate ownership were curtailed, the value of real estate declined. In that case, the resulting loss of value in the commercial real estate sector was 30 percent.

EXPERT'S VIEW

Explains Doug Duncan, chief economist for the Mortgage Bankers Association, "Quite simply what will happen is that the interest expense for borrowing money will rise and that will reduce demand; so, the demand side will fall. Second, the value of the tax deduction is capitalized into the price of the house. When it is removed, the house price will fall by the capitalized value of that deduction."

It is hard to estimate the specific value, but some economists suggest between 10 and 20 percent.

Any way you look at it—it's a tax increase.

EXPERT'S VIEW

Lawrence Yun, senior economist with the NAR says, "Consumer spending is two-thirds of the gross domestic product, and it's been the rising home prices that have supported that. A plunge of 15 percent in home prices would be devastating. It could put the economy into a recession. It could have severe effects and could put a lot of lenders underwater because the collateral value is below the loan amount. It would put financial institutions under stress, and the effects could last for quite some time."

People who do not have mortgages or who pay low property taxes might not be hurt, but this may not be the best way to evaluate the situation. Explains Yun, "If you have two identical homes for sale on the same street, one being sold by a person who itemizes and the other being sold by a person who doesn't itemize, it is inconceivable that the home prices will be different because the owner itemizes or doesn't itemize. The owners who don't itemize will lose appreciation too."

Yet, the panel appeared unswayed. Treasury Secretary John Snow said he did not know what ideas the administration would embrace after the Treasury made its recommendations. (Keep a lookout for this information. Just because it's a dormant issue today, doesn't mean it won't be resurrected tomorrow.)

Elimination of Property Tax Deductions

Eliminating the deductions for local real estate taxes (i.e., property taxes) would have an even broader impact—reaching those who own their homes free and clear in addition to those who still have a mortgage. Retirees are particularly affected since many of them own their homes outright and the property tax deduction is one of the few deductions they can take. Living on a fixed income, the elimination of this deduction would be a significant added expense that many retirees could not afford. It also particularly impacts residents of states with especially high property taxes.

Steve Cook, vice president of public affairs for NAR, expects a long, loud debate over any housing tax reforms. A change in tax benefits for homeowners makes housing more expensive for everyone. "It's a middle-class tax incentive," Cook explains. "If you are worth a lot, it doesn't mean that much—but it means a lot to the middle class." Interestingly enough, there is not a single economic think tank, government agency, or academic research laboratory that has any data on what the loss of tax incentives would do to housing or how the loss of such an incentive would impact on the economy.

That's a scary thought.

HOUSING PRICE/EARNINGS RATIO (P/E)

A favorite "shorthand" measure for stocks is the price/earnings ratio (P/E)—what the stock costs versus what it is earning per share. The higher the price to earnings, the more overvalued the stock, and vice versa.

Some economists suggest that the P/E for housing should be determined by "combining the flow-of-funds data on residential real estate values with the National Income and Product Accounts data (gathered by the Bureau of Economic Analysis [BEA])—the consumption of housing services." This is measured by calculating what renters pay and what homeowners would pay in rents should they rent from themselves. The rentals could be thought of as the earnings of the housing "stock," adjusted for appreciation.

By that measure, the P/E of national housing has gone from 14/8 (price to earnings) in 1960 to 20/2 (price to earnings) in early 2005. Housing has gone up at a compound rate of 8.5 percent. In the last 45 years, housing receded in price in only six quarters. The most severe price recession occurred in the first quarter of 1993, when housing sank $19 billion. However, according to BEA, it was quickly made up by "a whopping $113 billion increase the following quarter."

When housing prices rise too much, they eventually become unaffordable for home buyers. Inventory sits, allowing rents the chance to absorb the stagnant inventory.

As an example, the BEA research goes back to 1979 through 1986 when inflation was rampant and affordability dropped to record levels. Housing turnover fell 55 percent between 1978 and 1982, yet prices continued to rise. This suggested that the housing turnover was at least "twice as sensitive as housing prices to fluctuations in interest rates and cyclical variables like unemployment."

That is why inventory tends to swell at first and then shrink, as homeowners take their homes off the market and wait for more favorable conditions. The BEA concludes that "equities stand out as remarkably expensive in the 1990s; or to put it differently, housing looked cheap in the 1990s. Perhaps this helps to explain its recent, sharp outperformance."

Joint Center for Housing Studies at Harvard University

Housing economists at Harvard see housing P/Es a little differently. Instead of comparing prices and earnings as rent, "The State of the Nation's Housing: 2005" economists used a different metric: price of homes to the income needed to buy them.

The report found that the "ratios of house prices to median household incomes were up sharply and then stood at a 25-year high in more than half of the evaluated metro areas. Indeed, the number of metros where the median house price-to-income ratio was at least four had more than tripled from 10 to 33 in the past five years." These high-priced markets, mostly in southern California, New York City, and southern Florida, house about one-quarter of the nation's households.

However, the report found that prices were not as bleak as they sounded. Seventy-seven of the 110 markets covered in the study had price-to-household-income earnings of less than four. The amount borrowed to buy a home was still well within the classic lender guidelines of 28 percent of the buyers' gross income used for housing, and 36 percent of the gross income when including other debt.

Do high P/Es stop people from buying overvalued stocks?

California Dreamin'

You may notice that a lot of national housing news seems to center around California. There's a very good reason for that.

According to the U.S. Department of State's Bureau of International Information Programs, 10 percent of the U.S. population resides in California. One out of every nine Americans is a Californian, and by 2006, one out of every eight U.S. residents will live there. It is the most populous state in the union, as well as the most urban. It also has one of the lowest affordability rates in the country—an all-time low of 15 percent. That means that only 15 percent of Californians—the ones who make $128,270 or more—can afford a median-priced home, priced at $543,980. As of November 2005, that was three times the amount needed to buy a median home in the rest of the United

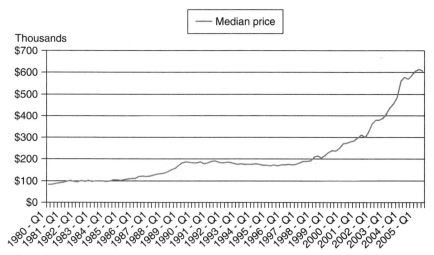

FIGURE 5.1 *San Diego Home Price*
Source: National Association of REALTORS®

States. The housing market in California has seen double-digit increases for four years, which suggests to some that it is certainly booming. (See Figure 5.1.)

EXAMPLE

To give you an idea of how popular it has become to live in California, in 1968 the median home cost $23,210. The median home in the United States cost $20,100.

Difference: 15.5 percent higher in California than the U.S. median

By 1999, the median California home was $217,510 while the median U.S. home was $133,300.

Difference: 63.2 percent higher

By 2004, the median California home had more than doubled to $450,990, while the U.S. median home had merely skyrocketed to $185,200.

Difference: 143.5 percent higher!

Out Migration Is Greater Than Foreign Immigration

While California is still the nation's most populous state at 35.9 million (2004), it loses more residents to other states than it gains in foreign immigration. In fact, it has been losing population for years. The U.S. Census Bureau has noted that many fast-growing states such as Nevada and Arizona were attracting Californians, 755,000 of whom migrated between 1995 and 2000. California was the nation's fifth fastest-growing state during the 1980 to 1990 period, but dropped to the nineteenth position during the 1990 to 1994 period. Its population is still growing, but the rate of growth has declined each year since 1990, and its 1993 to 1994 growth rate of 0.7 percent was well below the national average of 1.0 percent, according to the Bureau.

The reason? California home buyers flee high home prices. California has a large enough population so that it spills into other states, especially when prices get out of reach for some home buyers. Others want to cash in their housing chips and place their winnings in Las Vegas, Scottsdale, or other cities. Leslie Appleton-Young, chief economist for the California Association of REALTORS® (CAR), says that, anecdotally speaking, one-third of the relocating families going to Las Vegas are from California.

A decade ago, while recovering from a number of earthquakes, fires, floods, and a horrific housing recession, equity-rich Californians poured their money into much-cheaper Texas. They brought such novelties as "spa cuisine" and bottled-water slings with them. So, what happens in California does indeed matter to the rest of the nation.

For example, the state is reporting double-digit appreciation of home prices for its 2006 forecast, yet affordability in the state has hit new lows. If affordability is too low for most to be able to afford homes, why is California still booming? Because demand is there—low interest rates, exotic loans, tax benefits, and wealthy home buyers. California grows by 230,000 to 250,000 households annually, a growth rate of about 1.5 percent. Baby Boomers, those aged 41 to about 67, account for about 40 percent of the market and will continue to impact sales and afford-ability, says CAR. With the first of the Baby Boomers turning 60 this year, their impact is likely to drive California prices even higher.

The most important reason for buying, according to CAR, is the desire to stop renting, cited by nearly 49 percent of first-time buyers. Investment/tax reasons for buying were cited by 13 percent, and 11 percent purchased because they wanted a "better location." Higher prices forced first-timers to borrow 33 percent more money in their first mortgages than last year, or to take on a second mortgage—actions that increased 36.4 in 2003 and 57.2 percent in 2004. Down payments dropped 27.6 percent to $18,450.

EXPERT'S VIEW

"What jumped out at me," said CAR's chief economist Leslie Appleton-Young, "was that the percentage of first-time buyers was low, 26 percent—that's the lowest that number has been since 1979. It's a testament of the affordability hurdles that first-timers face and the 22 percent price appreciation—the highest since 1979." These figures look like a perfect real estate storm brewing, but she feels that home buyers will not stop buying. They will likely sub-stitute homes they want for homes they can afford; even if that means moving inland or out of state.

It is expected that the median home price in California will increase 10 percent to $575,500 in 2006, compared with a projected median of $523,150 in 2005. Sales for 2006 are projected to reach 630,610 units, falling 2 percent compared with 2005.

The last time affordability was so low, California housing lost value and took years to recover. According to *Local Market Monitor*, Los Angeles homes topped the market at $220,200 in 1990. By 1996, homes were worth $176,300, a 20 percent loss. If homes had been adjusted for inflation, they would have lost more than 34 percent of their value, according to CNN. However, California home prices rebounded as much as 103 percent in the last five years, even though affordability reached a record low.

Housing Forecast

In the November 2005 edition of *The Campbell Real Estate Timing Newsletter*, investment advisor Robert Campbell wrote, "Creative financing can be very dangerous when the price of the asset loses significance. People start believing that it does not matter whether a home sells for $200,000 or $400,000, as the monthly payment is the same. Sorry, but when mortgage loans are based on fictional values as opposed to true values that are supported by economic fundamentals, financial bubbles can develop that eventually implode."

Markets always revert to their mean or true economic value, whether they are overvalued or undervalued. Vital signs to look for are:

- Existing home sales
- New home-building permits
- Notices of default
- Foreclosure sales
- Interest rates

Yet, that's not all bad. When overinflated asset prices fall to P/E ratios below long-term norms, that's a great buying opportunity. California homes have always sold for a significant premium compared

---

EXPERT'S VIEW

The price of homes is compared in a ratio with the income needed to buy them. In California, homes are at a price-to-income ratio of over 9/4—an extreme overvaluation by Campbell's calculations: "The California real estate market is now a bubble. Housing prices have risen to a price/earnings ratio that is significantly out of balance with sustainable economic fundamentals."

---

to other U.S. homes: 63 percent more than other homes in other states since 1968. In September 2005, the median U.S. home was $212,000. The same home in California should cost $345,560 (212,000 × 63 percent = 133,560 added to 212,000 = $345,560). If the median home in California is $544,000, and the national median home is $212,000, the California market is overpriced by $199,000, by historical standards.

With market bottoms in 1983 and 1996, the market premiums were 63 percent and 50 percent, for an average of 57 percent. That means the current market would have to drop 39 percent to meet that lowest average. Using a 38-year historic norm, housing prices would have to drop 36 percent to $346,000. However, it is unlikely that with today's easy credit, investors, speculators, and home buyers would ever let the real estate market get that low again.

Viva Las Vegas

From mid-2003 to mid-2004, Las Vegas, Nevada, experienced an eye-popping 52 percent appreciation, fueling as much flipping, speculation, and gold-rushing as the area would allow. The fact that many of those home buyers came from California drew even more attention to the boom.

There are plenty of reasons to think that Las Vegas continues to lead the housing boom. NAR's "bubble report" found that, like other suspects, housing prices have risen faster in Las Vegas than the area family incomes. Home values have risen 88 percent against a national average of 32 percent over the last three years. The home price-to-income ratio is 3/4, whereas the national average is 2/3.

While incomes relative to housing prices are certainly important, the NAR considers that a more important measure in assessing housing bubbles is mortgage servicing costs relative to income. In other words, are borrowers overstretched to purchase a home in the area? In Las Vegas, the mortgage debt servicing cost is 25 percent of income. While higher than the national average of 16 percent, it is well below the Top 20 metros' servicing cost of 30 percent of income.

More than 175,000 jobs have been created in the valley in the last five years. Simultaneously, the region added 170,000 units of housing, of which 140,000 units were single-family homes. This means that the housing-to-job-creation ratio is above one. It appears that Las Vegas is very healthy.

However, demand is causing prices to rise. Las Vegas homes priced at $300,100 are 40 percent above the national average. The median home price rose 46.4 percent in 2004. Home prices may be "catching up" from flat pricing for most of the 1980s and 1990s. Only 12 percent of loans had a loan-to-value ratio greater than 90 percent, which implies minimal foreclosure risk. There is just as much reason to suspect that Las Vegas is in a boom, not a bubble, with a 12 percent increase in the number of jobs created, compared to a national average of about 2 percent.

> **EXPERT'S VIEW**
>
> *With between 5,000 and 7,000 people moving to Las Vegas every month, there is a continued demand for housing—that squares with NAR chief economist David Lereah's assessment. "These market fundamentals, combined with relatively tight inventories of available land and homes available for sale in southern Nevada, mean there is solid demand from buyers compared to the supply of homes."*

Las Vegas has set consecutive growth records for over 18 years. "It would take drastic alterations in the southern Nevada economy, such as a reversal of the area's strong growth in population, tourism, jobs, and the overall economy, to change that growth pattern," says Greater Las Vegas Association of REALTORS' president Myrna Kingham.

That does not mean that Las Vegas housing will not plateau, or even recede for a while, but as long as people want to move there, and as long as there are jobs to support families, there will be a market for housing. The NAR's "stress test" for a market decline in Las Vegas is 5 percent. Those stressors would include mortgage interest rates escalating to 8 percent with job losses of 152,000, or 9 percent with job losses of 108,000. Instead, NAR anticipates that Las Vegas will create more than 50,000 jobs over the next 24 months, and interest rates will rise to about 7 percent.

CHAPTER
6

AFTER THE BOOM, BUBBLE, AND BUST

Waiting Out a Buyers' Market

When the wind dies, and buyers stop coming around, it takes a few months for sellers to get the message that they are not going to get what they thought they would for their homes. Once a buyers' market begins, sellers count the days until the market turns again, and buyers start showing up for open houses, talking to lenders, and making their plans to move. How quickly and deeply sellers start discounting their homes depends on how desperate they are to get out of their homes.

If you have owned property for just a few years, the odds are overwhelming that in most areas—but not all—you are ahead of the game. According to the NAR, the national median existing single-family home price was $213,000 in the fourth quarter of 2005, up 13.6 percent from a year earlier when the median price was $187,500. That's up considerably from $139,000 in 2000.

EXAMPLE

In other words, if you bought five years ago and sold today at a 15 percent discount from the September (2005) top, the property would still close at $180,200. You would be ahead by $31,800 before closing costs. If you bought with 10 percent down in 2000, and you put up $13,900 plus closing costs, you would have doubled your money or come close. That is not a bad deal when you see that the Dow Jones Industrial Average went from 10462.00 on November 20, 2000, to 10766.33 on November 18, 2005. And it is surely not a bad deal in the face of inflation, according to "Realty Times" columnist Peter Miller.

Of course, in many areas, the gains are much larger. This has almost all sellers fantasizing about the use for this newly found wealth: to pay off equity loans used to send kids to college, take a cruise, or pay off credit card debt. Unfortunately, none of this adds value to their real estate.

WHAT HOME SELLERS CAN DO

The first rule of selling is that a home can contribute to your retirement and money management. However, there is not a buyer on Earth who will pay you for your financial goals. Just like you, they want a home they can convey at a profit. So, if you have taken an equity loan for any purpose other than to improve your home, do not feel entitled to get that money back from a buyer.

The second rule of selling is that a home will not sell for more than the market will bear. The market is a *state of mind* made more positive or more negative based on economics; perceived quality of life; good local schools; nearby services, shopping, and jobs; and many other things. One compromise on any lifestyle or economic front can cause buyers to pull back and wait for better terms. That is not the time to price your home to pay for your retirement without considering what buyers want and whether your home can deliver it.

In any market, the homes that sell first and for the most money are the ones that offer the best presentation to the marketplace, are fairly priced in line with the current market, and offer alluring incentives to buyers. (See Figure 6.1.)

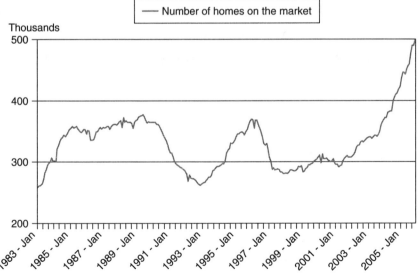

FIGURE 6.1 *New-Home Inventory*
Source: U.S. Census Bureau

Prepare Your Home to Sell

You have two areas of competition to consider:

- New homes that can be customized and built or that are move-in ready with warranties and incentives
- Homes in your own neighborhood that have undergone updates that bring the property to today's standards. Such updates would include new kitchens and baths with granite countertops, stainless appliances, new cabinetry, and designer accents, for example. However, do not expect to make a profit on everything you do, particularly on foundation repairs, new roofs, gutters, sidewalk repair, etc. There is a difference between routine maintenance and home improvement.

To get an idea of the competition, take a tour of a new-home community and evaluate the homes. You might see more space, better floor plans, finer finishes, and more expensive appliances than you offer in your home. But that does not mean your home cannot compete with a new home. Your neighborhood may be more established, where people know what they are buying. You can refresh and update your home to offer many of the same amenities as a new home, but in a charming, older neighborhood near city amenities.

Be aware of buyers' pet peeves:

- Dirt, smells, wear, and other signs of biological use or neglect of the home
- Clutter, clutter, clutter
- Sellers overvaluing their homes for reasons buyers could care less about
- Obvious repairs and updates that need to be made

Most buyers want a home they can move right into without so much as picking up a broom. In addition, buyers are easily distracted because they are looking at a lot of homes.

Stage the house as if it were a model home that anyone could own. Pictures of yourself and your family should be taken down; they only show buyers that the house belongs to somebody else. Personalization is an individual right, but you want to "depersonalize" for your buyer to allow him or her to imagine personal belongings in the home.

Clutter is not only distracting, it suggests a kind of carelessness and tendency to procrastinate that may make the buyer suspect that you are not really ready to sell, or worse, that you have been too lazy or busy to do regular maintenance in the home. A tidy place suggests you are ready to make a deal and move out on a moment's notice. (Pay particular attention to rooms that typically collect clutter, like garages and attics. Clean those out first!)

Pay attention to detail. It is not enough to fix the big stuff like the roof and the plumbing, but ignore the pet stain on the rug. The most ardent dog-lover will not want to deal with another pet's stains. Cooks will not like kitchen drawers that stick. The less the buyer has to consider to fix or to budget for, the more likely your home will be chosen to move into.

Think white-glove test to prove move-in readiness.

Work with Buyers to Move Your Home

Perhaps your home is in a market that is receding from a record high. It is natural to think that your home is still worth the same amount as it was a year ago; but the market has changed. Suddenly, there are more homes for sale, and buyers can be choosy. Pride will keep you from selling your home if you do not adjust your price or terms to compete in the current market.

The easy answer, of course, is not to sell. Wait for the market to return to previous highs, which history suggests will happen in most markets. But even if you do not have that option, it does not mean you have to slash the price of your home. Instead, *offer better terms* to buyers.

Seller's Contribution One of the things you can do is offer a seller's contribution to the buyer in the form of down payment assistance or assisting with the buyer's closing costs. Many buyers would prefer to keep their cash or use it for other things, such as buying furniture or making improvements. That's a wonderful incentive you can offer that will bring a larger pool of buyers to your home rather than someone else's.

As a seller, you can also offer to pay some of the buyer's closing costs, such as pay the points (discount points) on the loan so the buyer can obtain a lower interest rate.

EXPERT'S VIEW

"Imagine that a home is priced at $550,000 and has remained unsold for several months. One option is surely to reduce the price. But a 3 percent seller contribution means a buyer would need $16,500 less at closing—and a 3 percent seller contribution may be a better option for sellers than a 5 or 10 percent price reduction," says Peter Miller, columnist for Realty Times. *"Lenders routinely allow seller contributions without regarding them as a pricing discount. This is important because mortgages are made as a percent of the sale price or the appraised value, whichever is less. Some loan programs allow as much as a 3 percent seller contribution, others go as high as 6 percent and some may go higher,"* he says.

Rent to Own Another way to save buyers down payment money is to allow them to "rent to own." In this agreement, a portion of the rental payment goes toward establishing a down payment to purchase the home eventually. The term *rent to own* is another way of saying "lease option." Buyers are better able to understand rent to own because they may already be renting their apartment and furniture.

EXPERT'S VIEW

"When you package a rent-to-own program, you are getting the premium selling price, because you are also "selling" financing. You will sell to people who cannot qualify for a normal mortgage, so it will be a different type of sale," says Diane Kennedy, CPA and coauthor of The Insider's Guide to Real Estate Investing Loopholes *(Wiley, 2005).*

WHAT HOME BUYERS CAN DO

Whether you are buying a place to live in or to invest in, you can make money several ways, but the first way is to buy *right* in the first place. The key is to buy properties that move well in *any* market. When a seller's market rises, it lifts all boats. If you buy a property that is marginal in condition or location, expect it to increase in value, but not to the extent more "desirable" properties would. If the market turns worse, marginal houses are more difficult to unload.

In *Trump Strategies for Real Estate*, George H. Ross, one of Donald Trump's advisors, identifies three keys to Trump's phenomenal success:

1. Acquire at a bargain purchase price.
2. Visualize the profit potential that nobody else sees.
3. Pull everything together, no matter how long it takes.

Savvy investors like Trump also force more market value by adding profitable improvements.

There are two ways to profit as a buyer in real estate—flipping for short-term appreciation gain or holding property for long-term equity gain. You can buy a fixer-upper to flip. Or, you can purchase a new home and flip it once it is built, with the intention of finding a buyer who wants a move-in-ready home. But that works best in a sellers' market. You can also purchase a home and move into it or rent it, with long-term appreciation in mind. That works in either a buyers' or sellers' market.

Flip Property

To flip effectively, you need to buy either in a quickly appreciating neighborhood or a market next door to a hot market so that you can catch the spillover buyers. Move-in-ready improvements are essential, especially with an older home. Kitchens and baths must have the latest: granite counters, stainless appliances, or whatever is hot at the moment. For less expensive properties, save the wine coolers and specialty upgrades.

New homes often come with rules against flipping, so pick your builder and/or community Home Owners Association well. If you can, make sure you are one of the first to buy so you can be the first to sell. Wait until the community is sold out to flip the property, so you do not have to compete with the lower builder prices. Keep your transaction costs in mind so you know for certain that you are going to make a profit. (You will make more if you do not move into the property.)

Hold Property

Buying and holding property is a more sure-footed way to capitalize on appreciation. If you rent the home right away, make sure you are getting enough rent to cover your reserves (money set aside for repairs and improvements). Renting at a loss only works in a market where homes are appreciating faster than rents are going up.

If you move into the home, only make improvements or upgrade selections from the builder that average homeowners want in your price range. It is not smart to overimprove for any given neighborhood, unless market momentum is on your side and you see others in your area upgrading their homes. While living in the house, do what any home-owner would do to maintain and grow the value of the property—from replacing and repairing failing fixtures to brightening the ambiance with fresh paint, good interior design, and landscaping.

If you have purchased a property as an investment, you can do all of the above—and then some. Be prepared to perform the duties of a property manager or, at minimum, be willing to pay a Realtor/property manager to function in your stead. Someone must collect rent, pay bills, provide routine maintenance, and deal with tenants—activities that you may not have the time to do or the expertise to handle.

Be Aware of Buyer Paralysis

If you wait so long to buy that you become paralyzed by the things that can go wrong instead of what can go right, you will never get the chance to profit. If you continue to let one great home after another pass you by, it is time to ask yourself why you are unable to make a decision.

Buying a home can be an overwhelming process. It is your greatest financial debt, even while it puts a roof over your head. Homes need repairs and maintenance, and they can go down in value, as well as up. With all that weighing on you, you could have "commitment-phobia." Maybe it is time to focus on the quality of life that a home can provide and worry a little less about the investment aspect. There are plenty of specific advantages, such as tax breaks, rising real estate values, and a stable environment for your family—to name only a few.

Here are the most typical home-buyer fears and what you can do to overcome them.

Fear of Spending Too Much Lenders will lend you money at the top of your ability to borrow. Realtors will suggest that you will be happier in a "bigger, better" home, eliminating the need to "trade up" in a few years. (See Figure 6.2.) Stretching to buy the most home you can possibly afford is a good strategy, but only under certain conditions:

- You have confidence that your salary will rise.
- Your income is stable.
- You can handle large surprise expenses.

Make yourself more comfortable with purchasing a home by budgeting some reserves. This means you might be more comfortable buying less—a less expensive home or a home in a less expensive neighborhood.

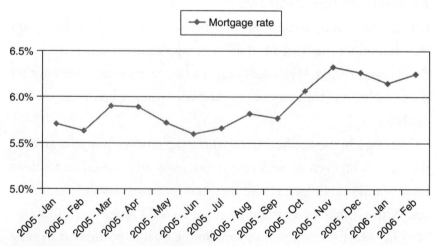

FIGURE 6.2 *Rising Mortgage Rates*
Source: Freddie Mac

Many financial advisors tell their clients to budget about 25 percent of their income for housing in order to position them to contribute to savings, investments, and emergencies. That is almost 6 percent less than lenders will allow you to borrow. Just think what else you can do with 6 percent of your income. You will still have your house, plus money for other things.

Conflict in Goals If you are trying to accomplish two big financial goals at the same time, such as buying a home and adding to your family, or paying off a student loan, or starting a business, then prepare to sacrifice some peace of mind. A better alternative may be to prioritize your goals. In what order of importance do you want your life to move forward?

Concern with Cash Flow If you are worried about cash flow, making disproportionately large house payments will tarnish the joy of home ownership, unless you can find ways to cut down your other debts. You have to work to improve your cash flow. Accelerate your credit card payoffs. Do not incur new debt. Rebudget your expenses and eliminate unnecessary expenditures. Make compromises: vow to cut down if you cannot cut something out. Be willing to move timelines for meeting your goals. Do not be influenced by others to live beyond your means. Set your sights on an *affordable* home.

Fear of the Future Fear takes the fun out of a lot of things, but there is reasonable fear *and* unreasonable fear. Unreasonable fears have no basis in reality. You can handle reasonable fears on your own with a little common sense.

What if we cannot make our payments? What if you manage your money so well you can make double payments? *It's about controlling your money.* Ask someone whose money management style you admire for advice on how to manage your money better. Then stick with it.

What if the value of our home goes down? What if your property value goes up? You can mitigate some devaluation by proper maintenance and adding enhancements. Build cash reserves to perform scheduled and unscheduled maintenance. Look at the properties surrounding the home you are considering. Are they maintained with pride? Do homes sell quickly in the area because of high demand? Then your chances are good that the neighborhood and your home will retain its value. Rest assured that there will always be a buyer for an attractive, well-maintained property. Real estate is not as volatile as you think. Your best hedge against the future is to keep your property in desirable condition over the long term.

What if . . . ? You cannot predict the future. The only thing you can do is prepare yourself to handle what may happen. Wait a few days or weeks if you need to. Use the time to regroup and think smaller and/or less expensive. It is far better for you to work through a few obstacles than to jump into the largest investment of your life without the confidence you need to carry it through. If you can work through your fears, get your finances in tip-top shape and proceed. You will find that buying a home can be one of the most exhilarating things you will ever do.

The Better-Deal Buyer

Real estate produces wins and losses, but there are also lose-lose or win-win situations. How well the transaction goes depends not only on the terms, but on the behavior of the principals. You want the best deal possible, but if you are willing to risk a good deal because you are not winning every negotiating point, you may be more interested in feeding your ego than buying a house. That's the *better-deal buyer.*

The better-deal buyer is always looking for a better agent, a better loan, or a better house. Better-deal buyers lose great home-buying opportunities for various reasons:

The interest rate was too high. Unless you shop several lenders at exactly the same time of day on the same day, rates can change. The rate you were quoted an hour ago might not be good anymore.

The house did not have the right features. You want a bargain, but you want the house to be in perfect repair, in the best neighborhood, and priced below what it's worth. (You're probably not going to find this one.) A true bargain is when others do not see the possibilities, but you do. So, instead of complaining to the sellers that their 60-year-old house does not have the features of today's homes, look at the home's possibilities. Can a wall be knocked out? Can that floor be replaced? To get a bargain, you are going to have to think creatively of how the space can be improved for better use.

The price wasn't right. Sellers can be a little proud of their homes, just like you will be when it comes time for you to sell. Do not get angry. Get the price down by showing sensible comparables for what the home is worth.

WHAT BETTER-DEAL BUYERS CAN DO

If you are the buyer, you want to buy at the lowest price and for the best terms that you possibly can. As a seller, you also want the highest price and best terms. That is why a real estate negotiation is not much different than a game of cards. You are not going to win every hand, but with some smart strategizing, you can do quite well with real estate.

It's a matter of how much you want to stake in the game.

One strategy is to buy a more expensive house.

EXPERT'S VIEW

"A 10 percent appreciation rate creates $10,000 of wealth for a $100,000-priced home, but $20,000 of wealth for a $200,000-priced home," David Lereah writes in Are You Missing the Real Estate Boom? *(Century, 2005). What this means is that a higher-priced home provides greater return. It also creates a "forced savings" in higher payments that you get back in the form of interest rate and property tax deductions.*

However, more modestly priced homes are also expected to rise in value over the next decade because of increasing lack of affordability. There is nothing wrong with pocketing a modest profit for a modest investment.

If you stick with the real estate mantra—location, location, location—think about what assets are important in your area. In some communities, properties near good transportation or schools do well. Think of views, tranquility, and attractive neighborhoods. Beware of communities with one or two major employers. Look for diversified local economies.

Use your loan wisely. If you plan on living in your home for only a few years, buying a more expensive home with an adjustable-rate mortgage makes sense, but if you plan on a longer term, a fixed-rate mortgage is best.

Your Home and Tax Benefits

In the last few years, many have thought of their homes as a built-in savings plan, especially when they are able to sell and enjoy profits without paying capital gains.

Diane Kennedy, real estate tax authority, suggests four ways for making your home pay its own way:

1. *Depreciation.* If a portion of your home is used for a home office or other business use, you have a choice to depreciate a pro-rata portion of your home. This depreciation will go to offset business income.

2. *Unforeseen circumstances.* If you have lived in your home for two of the previous five years, you will get a tax-free capital gains exclusion of $500,000 for married couples or $250,000 for singles. The unforeseen circumstances situation will allow you to get a partial exclusion even when you spend less than two years in a home due to a corporate transfer or some other event.

3. *Mortgage interest rate deduction.* Most get to take advantage of this, but you are limited to a total acquisition indebtedness of $1 million for your principal and secondary residence. If you find you are subject to alternative minimum tax (and it's estimated that 3 million more taxpayers will be subject to this tax next year), you will lose even more of the deduction.

4. *Property taxes.* Property taxes are always deductible, right? Wrong! Watch out for alternative minimum tax reductions.

A tax credit, unlike a tax deduction that reduces your taxable income, actually directly reduces the tax you pay. Some examples of real estate tax credits include:

- *Low-income housing.* Check with your local government for qualification. Typically these are awarded by your local government.
- *Rehabilitation credit.* Historic and pre-1936 construction can qualify for 10 percent tax credit on improvements made.
- *ADA improvements.* You get up to a 50 percent tax credit for work you perform on your business space to make it accessible to persons with disabilities under the Americans with Disabilities Act (ADA) guidelines. There is an annual limit to how much you can take in this tax credit. Currently you're limited to just a little over $10,000 with a 50 percent tax credit. The rest of the credit is rolled into the next year. (It is not a deduction against taxable income.)

Is this a great country, or what?

The Rental Outlook

With 36 percent of properties purchased in 2004 and 2005 by "investors" and second-home buyers, it is certain that a large number of these and other properties will find their way into the rental pool. However, in a low-interest, easy money environment, many rental candidates opt to buy their own properties, taking the most qualified tenants out of the equation. Continued low interest rates and special loan packages can exacerbate low returns in the rental market. As interest rates rise, that changes and affordability issues knock some potential home buyers back into the rental pool.

Anything wrong with building equity by having someone else make your house payment for you?

Since World War II, house prices and rental prices increased at roughly the same rate or ahead of inflation, according to the Bureau of Labor Statistics. However, recently, record increases in housing prices (more than 45 percent after adjusting for inflation over the last eight years) have left rents behind. Further depressing rents was new construction brought on by attractive subsidies and loans. Rental vacancy rates have climbed nationally for five consecutive years (mirroring the house-buying boom). According to the report, "State of the Nation's Housing: 2006," by Harvard's Joint Center for Housing Studies, vacancies have slowly reversed, with more rental markets showing improvement than the last two years combined.

The rental market for *single-family homes* improved 47 percent from 1993 to 2003, but peaked at 37.5 percent in the 1990s. This resulted from steady corporate relocations that allowed transferees to lease executive homes rather than buy and resell in a year with unpredictable gains in equity. But rental costs can also be unpredictable. With interest rates moving higher, that puts more pressure on home buyers and that means an increase in rentals; but higher interest rates also mean higher costs to service debt for landlords. This simultaneously makes home ownership more unaffordable and renting more attractive, but not necessarily for landlords unless rents rise enough to make it more attractive for home seekers to rent than to buy.

Clear as mud?

RENTAL DEMOGRAPHICS

The Joint Center for Housing Studies of Harvard University says diversity has hit the rental market too. From 1993 to 2003, the minority share of renters has jumped from 31 to 43 percent, fueled by record immigration. Immigrants headed 16 percent of all renter households and nearly 30 percent of all minority renter households. While more whites have become homeowners, immigrant and minority renters have filled the vacuum, raising rental rates for landlords across many markets *and all housing types.*

More renters, like home buyers, are moving to the Sunbelt states, with the number of renter households rising by 800,000 between 1993 and 2003. There, they are running into possibly higher rents, fewer concessions, and more competition than they may be used to, particularly in apartment complexes and other affordable housing.

EXPERT'S VIEW

"With a record two-thirds of respondents noting tighter market conditions, I think it's time to say that the apartment market has completed its recovery," says National Multi Housing Council chief economist Mark Obrinsky. (That's a significant achievement in the face of two powerful headwinds: the surge in home ownership and the most sluggish job market recovery on record.)

DWINDLING RENTAL PROPERTIES CREATE OPPORTUNITY

Until all those adjustable-rate mortgages roll over, and speculators get ready to dump their inventory on the market, there is a tailwind to the rental market. Between 1993 and 2003, there were only enough new rental properties built to replace existing ones lost to "conversion, demolition, or abandonment," a net gain of about 1.2 million housing units over the decade. Many of those units are in areas that have seen a net decline in renter households, such as the South and Midwest.

But the replacement of older units has created a crisis in affordable rentals. Only 10 percent of rentals built since 2000 rent for less than $400 a month, compared with 25 percent of existing units. Thirty-one percent of renters have incomes under $16,000, which means that affordable rentals are disappearing at an alarming rate. The shortfall of affordable *and* available units is about 5.2 million. (Note: New apartments require an income of $32,000 to afford rents of $600 to $800 monthly.)

The upshot, says the Joint Center for Housing Studies, is that the home-buying boom has "held growth in renter households to near zero for the past 10 years, but Gen-Yers and aging Boomers will reignite the rental market. This could be extremely good for single-family homes, townhomes, condominiums, and other types of homeowner properties.

Why Housing Will Continue to Grow

It is a sure bet that people will do what they have always done—go on living, dying, marrying, divorcing, remarrying, having children, blending Brady Bunch families, caring for aging parents, emptying their nests, making and losing money, and relocating for new opportunities. Throughout these life changes, we buy and sell homes.

We believe that owning a home improves our quality of life. It can put us into or take us out of an environment that is essential to leading a rewarding lifestyle. It is lifestyles that create housing markets. Anything else we think—that housing numbers are produced by speculation or long-term investment—is pure guesswork, because we don't know what we do not know until all the facts are in. All we know is that the home-buying public continues to amaze the pundits.

SHORT-TERM PREDICTIONS

Who would have thought 10 years ago when you could hardly give condos away that they would outpace single-family home values by 2004? Who would have thought in a world of volatile oil and gas prices that American homes would be twice the size and volume of those in the 1950s?

Many worry that the outlook for housing is not good. What will happen when all those exotic loans change interest rates? Will lack of affordability cause the first-time home buyer to drop out of the market? Which markets will return to the "mean" and when? Most economists believe that housing will ease by 2007, and pick up again as the economy retrenches. A pause in the escalation of real estate is both natural and expected. That's the ebb and flow of economies. When an economy goes slack, it cuts jobs; and job cuts mean no growth. No growth means no inflation and interest rates come back down again, stimulating reinvestment. The trick is in knowing how long the cycle takes to swing back in the other direction.

Interest Rates

Freddie Mac vice president and chief economist Frank Nothaft said, "Looking back at 2005, a 30-year fixed-rate mortgage averaged just about the same as they did for the last two years. Since the 30-year fixed rate is the most popular mortgage product by far, these low rates helped the housing market set records for home sales and new construction over the last three years."

EXPERT'S VIEW

"Looking ahead, as mortgage rates rise, housing activity will ease somewhat. So although 2006 will not be another record-setting year, it will likely beat the previous record for home sales and new construction set in 2003. In other words, 2006 will be another busy year for the housing sector," says Nothaft.

The UCLA Anderson Forecast that came out in early December 2005 says that easy money will not flow in 2006 like it did in 2005. New mortgage applications are down. New and existing home sales are slipping, new construction of housing has plunged, and houses are staying on the market longer—suggesting that whatever boom there was was over at the national level by mid-year 2006.

But these are short-term predictions. Housing can take a breather and still be on an upward trend.

In fact, the Joint Center for Housing Studies says that in 2004, 87 percent of homeowners had 20 percent or more equity in their homes, and only 3 percent had less than 5 percent equity, suggesting that if home prices continue to rise, they will continue to prove to borrowers that housing is a good place to put little or no money down.

Housing Prices

According to the Mortgage Bankers Association reports in its housing and mortgage market analysis, "Housing prices have tended to appreciate faster in states with higher rates of population growth, higher rates of employment growth, and higher rates of personal income growth. Appreciation rates tend to be slower in states with higher delinquency and foreclosure rates. However, delinquency rates are more closely tied to rates of employment growth than housing price growth." The report points out that price declines do not occur in isolation. They are accompanied by reduction in employment and population growth rates, and in many cases, "an outright drop in employment and population."

In addition, income growth rates were depressed while home prices dropped. For example, Hawaii's decline in tourism and investment followed Japan's stagnant economy, leading to substantial out-migration in the late 1990s. In the early 1990s, California was hit by the defense sector cutbacks that also led to recession, out-migration, and housing price drops.

With market prices depending on supply and demand, availability is strengthened or weakened by the number of units that builders can bring to the market. Housing prices also depend on how quickly supply can meet demand. Supply-side variables, such as the cost of construction, land prices, and restrictive regulatory barriers like lot sizes, impact fees, or zero-growth moratoriums, can also impact housing. Towns such as San Diego and Boulder have kept values high by limiting new housing projects. That makes rising unsold inventory a primary measure of housing health.

By the second quarter of 2006, both new and existing housing inventories had risen, but were well below the buyers' market turning point of six months. With about 20 percent of permitted homes not started, builders can slow production to meet softening housing demand. In November 2005, National Association of Home Builders chief economist David Seiders said, "We're looking for a 5 or 6 percent decline in home sales next year, compared to 2005. No huge drop (in demand) is in the cards." It is likely that "an orderly, cooling process that will lead to somewhat lower home sales and production in the future" is underway, he suggests, and he was right. Home sales did slow through mid-2006, but home prices continued to rise by approximately 6 percent.

This confirms what NAR leading economist David Lereah believes—that home values and other real estate investments will climb through the end of the decade:

- There is no expected contraction in the number of households. Boomers are in their peak earning years, creating demand for second homes and retirement homes.
- Immigrant growth over the past 20 years will result in record numbers of home buyers.
- Gen-Yers will come of home-buying age.
- Minority home buyers will continue to increase.
- Home ownership costs will be reduced, at the closing level and at the property tax level.
- Interest rates will remain low to normal due to lack of inflation pressures.
- Job and income gains will continue.

This does not mean there will be equal opportunity in every state, community, and cul-de-sac. However, there should be plenty of money to be made as a homeowner or investor in some neighborhood in your town.

CHAPTER
7

MAKE THE CURRENT MARKET CONDITIONS WORK FOR YOU

And that is the key phrase: the *current* market conditions. While the past can be the precursor to future values, such as predicting that people will always want to live in New York City and San Francisco, there are many other conditions that also matter. Is the market creating new and better-paying jobs? Is the market "hot" compared to other nearby or not so nearby areas? Are city planners, developers, and builders reading the market correctly and providing the right incentives and types of housing to attract and build a robust, vital, and prosperous community?

These questions go on and on, but for your purposes—those of the first-time home buyer, the first-time investor, or perhaps the second-home buyer—you should know the answers to these questions.

Either your house is about to crumble before your eyes like something out of a horror film, or you are building equity faster than the sun comes up every day. Whether or not you believe there is a housing bubble, this book has been an attempt to help you understand housing markets so that you can make informed decisions about your specific situation.

No one buys real estate to lose money, but as we have discussed, making money is only one of the many pieces of the equation. There are many reasons people buy and sell homes:

To enjoy the tax benefits of owning and selling

To put their kids into the "right" schools

To experiment with a new lifestyle

To retire

The reasons for buying or selling a home are sometimes tragic ones: illness, divorce, foreclosure, or the death of a spouse. Other times, it's simply to pursue a dream.

The investment factor should be considered in each of these situations, but only in the context of a greater goal that you seek to accomplish. Any return that beats inflation is a good return. And even if you don't beat inflation, there are such enormous tax benefits (thanks to Uncle Sam) that you'll still come out ahead.

Pay Attention to the News, but Don't Let the "Bubbleistas" Scare You

As you've learned, there are a number of factors driving housing investment, the most important of which is lack of competition from better-paying alternatives that you can put your money into. What gives housing such an edge over stocks, for example, is that you can borrow up to 100 percent of your financing; pay over long, comfortable periods; and enjoy all the appreciation. Even if your house were to lose money, which is unlikely (housing hasn't returned below-inflation rates since 1968), you still have the *use* of the asset.

Unlike businesses that you may invest in with the stock market, houses do not go bankrupt when they lose value; they are far more likely to recover and surpass former values, as was proven by the California and Texas markets. And, you can control this asset somewhat by what you see with your own eyes, rather than trusting the word of option-rich, performance-poor corporate governors. If your house needs paint, you paint it. Adding to this windfall are tax benefits in the form of mortgage interest rate deductions (so we get another benefit for borrowing as much as possible) and property taxes, which are income-tax deductible.

Since most people can enjoy these benefits, you have a population explosion of home buyers—and that is only sweetened by the wealth of aging Baby Boomers, for whom one house is not enough; the maturity of Gen X; and the coming of age of Gen Y. Add to that legal and illegal immigration, and you have a growing housing market all the way to 2050, as projected by the National Association of REALTORS®. If current housing sales are numbering above 7 million, by 2050, NAR anticipates 10 to 12 million homes will change hands annually. (See Table 7.1.)

Right now, we need to add 90 million housing units to the existing stock to meet the housing needs of 2050, says NAR. We need:

- 55 million units to house new people
- 15 million units to replace demolished units (this figure anticipates a low 0.2 percent depreciation rate or 300,000 housing unit demolitions annually)
- 20 million units to satisfy second-home purchases

HOUSING OUTLOOK

	2004	2005	2006
Existing-home sales	6.78 million	7.10 million	6.84 million
New-home sales	1.20 million	1.29 million	1.22 million
Housing starts	1.96 million	2.06 million	1.92 million
30-year floating-rate mortgages	5.8%	5.8%	6.5%
1-year adjustable-rate mortgage	3.9%	4.5%	5.3%
Existing-home price growth	9.3%	12.7%	6.1%

TABLE 7.1

Source: National Association of REALTORS®

The Harvard Joint Center for Housing Studies said in June 2006 that households will grow by over 2 million over the next 10 years, creating a demand for more housing.

But money is not the main driver of the American's desire to own a home. There is the emotional component that has been hardwired into the genes of this nation since we crossed the ocean centuries ago. To have a home of one's own in a free land is simply an irresistible concept—and it's highly achievable.

Where all these people choose to settle is what speculators and home buyers watch carefully. It's clear that the coasts are and will probably always be popular. They are immigrant entry points, but they also offer temperate climates through most coastal states, as well as attractive lifestyles.

Inland, people are creating their own lifestyles with planned communities that provide amenities that were unheard of only a few years ago: community pools, on-site nursing and hospital care, lake boating and fishing, and much more. People can tear down older homes and build McMansions because they are being rewarded for doubling and tripling the square footage of homes built half a century ago.

Housing is not only a way to build wealth, it is a way to live life the way you want, whether it's in an urban setting complete with bellhops and penthouse views, or in a single-family cottage in a neighborhood where everyone knows your name.

On the other hand, you have been warned by the financial press that the sky is about to fall, or that it's falling already, and there are some indicators that are worth paying attention to—but only if you consider them in context.

If builders overbuild, there will be sitting inventory that will bring down the prices of new and existing homes. But builders do not build to lose money. If they see that the market is sitting on the sidelines, they hold their inventory for better times. That is called the rate of absorption. As of May 2006, the rate of absorption nationwide was still well below six months of inventory on hand for both new and existing homes.

Interest rates are going up—that is true. As of March 2006, interest rates hit a 2½-year high. Out of context, that sounds fairly dire, doesn't it? But keep in mind that the *norm* for mortgage interest rates is much higher. After all, it is a long-term loan. Consider way back in 2000, when mortgage interest rates were just under 9 percent. Even if current rates rise to 7 percent, that is still less than mortgage interest rates that were charged back in 1972. (In 1981 through 1982, mortgage interest rates shot all the way up to nearly 17 percent.) Interest rates will impact buyers' ability to buy homes, but if they want homes of their own, they will do what buyers did in other higher-interest-rate periods—buy less house.

The federal government is trying to slow housing and may continue to raise short-term interest rates to banks, which in turn will impact mortgage interest rates. If the Fed is successful, housing will slow down. But it will still have enough momentum to match or exceed any of the record-breaking years of the new millennium because of the positive factors outlined above, and that is what is happening in 2006.

The point is that if you want to get into the market, don't worry about temporary fluctuations, as long as you have such positive economic indicators boosting your decision to own a home.

If you want to buy a home in California, where one out of eight will live, or settle in Florida, the state with the largest population over age 65 in the nation, there is no economic reason not to do so, except your fear that housing is overpriced. Because it cannot be proven one way or the other, you simply take your chances that you are doing the right thing.

10 Ways to Prosper from Buying and Selling Real Estate

1. **BUY RIGHT THE FIRST TIME.** There is something to be said for location, location, location. Do not buy the house next to the railroad track or the sewage treatment plant because it is cheap. It will always be cheap. Get as much safety, beauty, comfort, privacy, and convenience as you can within your means. (Know what's most important for you to have and what you are willing to sacrifice. If safety is more important to you than size, then go for it.)
2. **BUY FOR THE LONG HAUL.** Because of transaction costs as well as tax benefits, it makes sense to buy a home and stay in it for at least two years. If you want to rent it out later, you

can do so. If you do rent it out and hold the home for more than five years, you will lose your ability to sell the home without paying capital gains. However, your amortization schedule will kick in and with every passing year you will owe less on the home.

3. **KEEP YOUR HOME IN TOP CONDITION.** Set aside financial "reserves" for emergencies and normal maintenance like painting, appliance repair, carpentry work, chimney sweeping, and landscaping. This way, your home will always draw admirers because of its condition. As you learned earlier, there are three reasons homes sell: location, condition, and price.

4. **TREAT YOUR PROPERTY LIKE AN INVESTMENT, BUT MARKET IT LIKE A HOME.** You deserve a good home. That's a good enough reason to finish the home in ways that should be comfortable to you and appeal to the next home buyer. Buy a nice refrigerator that is comparable to what other homes in your area have. Don't skimp on window coverings. That is a dead giveaway to home buyers that you're either broke or trying to flip the house.

5. **USE EQUITY LOANS TO PAY FOR IMPROVEMENTS ON YOUR HOUSE (UNLESS IT IS AN EMERGENCY).** When home buyers look at your selling price, they want to see that you've put money into the home and brought the home up to market standards. If you spent the money on college for your kids or paying off credit cards, where is the value for the next buyer? Look at your home like you are running a business. If you take out an equity loan or home improvement loan, use it for the house.

6. **REFINANCE IF YOU ARE TRULY COMING OUT AHEAD.** All loans cost money; do not refinance to simply

get a lower interest rate. As long as interest rates are deductible, you may actually come out ahead by making your current payment and simply adding an extra $50 or $500 to the principal. (All loan coupons allow you to pay more toward your principal.)

7. **READ AND LISTEN TO THE NEWS, BUT CONSIDER THE SOURCE.** You are smart enough to know if a story is being hyped by the media. Double check what you are hearing against real data you can find through your local newspaper, Realtor association Web sites, and business journals.

8. **LEARN ABOUT PROPERTY MANAGEMENT.** If you are going to become a professional housing investor, you need to learn how to manage your money, how to choose properties, how to evict tenants, how to check credit reports and rent to new tenants without breaking fair housing laws, how to keep your property up to codes, and many other jobs. You should be able to attract good renters through advertising or special relationships with Realtors, lenders, and others and also keep them happy while they are using your home.

9. **ASSESS YOUR TOLERANCE FOR RISK.** It is very easy to become house poor, but it is also true that more expensive homes tend to hold their value better, mainly because wealthier people have more wherewithal to ride out financial storms. Plus, neighbors tend to stick together about keeping their home values up through outward appearances like fresh paint and new tulip bulbs. While it can be good advice for you to buy as much house as you possibly can, you will not enjoy being highly leveraged unless you have the risk tolerance for it. If you do not, simply buy less house and stick the difference in a savings account. Either way, you are building something— equity or cash—and neither one is bad.

10. **BE HONEST WITH YOURSELF ABOUT YOUR INTERESTS, ABILITIES, AND SHORTCOMINGS.** If you really want to make money on your property, you need to save money on it too. That means that you need to learn how to change air filters, unstop toilets, caulk bathtubs, water your foundation during droughts, landscape correctly so your yard drains properly, and hundreds of other home maintenance chores that will ultimately protect and enhance your home's value. Anything you do not want to do will go undone or have to be done by someone else for a fee. This is where a condominium might make more sense than a single-family home for some home buyers and investors.

Not everyone will be in a good position to buy or sell, and there's no advice that will create a miracle for you if you are in a less-than-ideal situation. But, no matter where you are in life, you are capable of making the smartest choice possible to improve your position.

Why?

Because now you understand how real estate markets work and *how you can make them work in your favor.*

A FINAL WORD

Like any other investment, real estate comes down to risk versus reward. If you want to make money with housing, you have to sift through the current data to spot opportunities, be willing to go against conventional wisdom, and do what others are unwilling to do: get there first. How do you do that? Skate to where you think the puck is going to be, not where it's going. Hockey legend Wayne Gretsky didn't know it, but when he revealed his strategy for success, he was giving great advice for real estate.

Let's say you want to build wealth through owning housing, but you do not quite know how to go about it. Start with learning the market conditions. Nearly 70 percent of Americans are homeowners. In the last two years, nearly 40 percent of the homes sold were to investors and second-home owners, and most of the loans provided last year were high-risk, low-entry adjustable-rate mortgages, which means that quite a number of people bought bigger, more expensive homes than they would have if their loans were fixed-rate.

If you think through what that means, a huge number of homes will be non-owner-occupied, with a strong leaning toward absorption in the high-end markets, leaving depressed older homes behind.

Now consider this: While buyers piled into luxury with their low-cost loans, there were record apartment conversions to condos, which depleted valuable workforce rentals. Condos overall appreciated faster than single-family homes last year. Unimproved older homes devalued in some areas, while in others affordable workforce housing was torn down, remodeled, or otherwise regentrified into luxury townhomes, high-rises, McMansions, or other high-priced housing.

Meanwhile, interest rates are rising; loans are tightening; the government is cooling housing through federal and legislative means; and the luxury party is coming to a temporary end.

What this means is too much money is chasing luxury homes, while a serious need for workforce housing is being unmet. And that spells opportunity. Is it smarter to buy more luxury housing at this point (with an adjustable rate) or take advantage of still-low fixed rates and buy affordable housing for rentals?

You could probably argue the case either way, but ask yourself, "Where is the puck, or opportunity, going to be?"

If you are going to make money at real estate, you have to get there first. Buy where the next boom is going to be. You are taking the risk that you are right, and if you are, the rewards will be higher than if you followed the crowd.

The alternative is to pay someone else a premium to take your risks for you, but that is just as risky. You do not want to buy at the top of the market because it could be years before the market reaches a new top and you can profit. While it seems counterintuitive, you have to be willing to do what others won't, and that is position yourself out there alone where you think the next big opportunity is going to be.

So, learn everything there is to know about property management and invest in older workforce housing near vital city centers and public transportation. Hold off on the gentrification, but make the properties clean, safe, pleasant, and livable to attract good tenants. Sit on the properties until they generate enough profit to buy more. Those semiluxury properties will become available one day, and many at a discount, so be ready to buy when others are desperate to bail out because they bought more than they could afford.

REAL ESTATE LANGUAGE

Adjustable-rate mortgage (ARM) A mortgage that permits the lender to adjust the interest rate periodically on the basis of changes in a specified index.

Amortization schedule A timetable schedule showing the amount of each payment applied to interest and principal and the remaining balance after each payment is made.

Appreciation Increase in the value of property.

Bankruptcy Federal court proceeding where a person with more debts than assets can reduce debts under a trustee's direction.

Blog Short for Weblog; journal (or newsletter) that is frequently updated and intended for general public consumption. Blogs generally represent the personality of the author or the Web site.

Bond Financial instrument that is issued for the purpose of raising capital by borrowing.

Buyers' market Exists when there are more homes for sale than buyers, giving buyers the negotiating advantage.

Capital gains Profit obtained from the sale of an asset, such as real estate.

Permission for some definitions was granted by the Real Estate Buyer's Agent Council of the National Association of REALTORS® at www.REBAC.net.

Condominium A housing structure of two or more units where the interior space is owned by the individual and the remaining space is owned in common by all individual owners of the units.

Consumer Price Index (CPI) Also called the Cost of Living Index; the increase or decrease of living costs for the average person on a monthly basis.

Cul-de-sac A street with an intersection at one end and a closed turning area at the other.

Depreciation The decline in the value of a property; opposite of appreciation.

Direct lender A mortgage lender of any size that makes loans from the lender's own portfolio of assets.

Down payment The initial amount of money a buyer will pay for a property, in addition to the money from a mortgage.

Due diligence Research that should be done in order to ensure that the property purchase can be as safe as possible.

Duplex Two residential units under one roof.

Economic bubble Speculation in a commodity causes the price to rise.

Economic indicators Governmental statistics released on a regular basis that indicate the growth and health of the country; the trade deficit, the gross national product (GNP), industrial production, the unemployment rate, and business inventories are some examples of economic indicators.

Equity A homeowner's financial interest in a property.

Escrow A deposit of value, money, or documents with a third party to be delivered upon the fulfillment of a condition. For example, the earnest money deposit is put into escrow and held by the broker, bank, or other party until delivered to the seller when the transaction is closed.

Exotic loans A reference to any of the available high-risk types of loans.

Fannie Mae (The Federal National Mortgage Association) A government-sponsored purchaser of loans in the secondary mortgage market.

Fixed-rate mortgage A mortgage where the interest and the payment remain the same for the term of the loan.

Flipping property Refers to the practice of acquiring real estate at substantially less than the market value and then reselling it quickly at full market value.

Foreclosure A legal process where a lender forces the sale of property because the borrower cannot make the mortgage payments.

Freddie Mac (Federal Home Loan Mortgage Corporation) Congressionally chartered institution that buys from lenders and resells them as securities on the secondary mortgage market.

Gross migration The sum of immigration and out-migration in an area during a specific period of time.

Home Owners Association An organization consisting of a group of owners who manage the common areas and set the rules; usually found in condominiums or closed communities.

Housing glut Situation where housing inventories in a given area are growing too fast for the amount of buyers that are available.

Hybrid loan products Any number of combinations of fixed- and adjustable-rate loans.

Index Products that are used to set interest rates for adjustable mortgage loans.

Inflation The upward price movement of goods and services in an economy.

In-migration Migration into an area for a certain period of time.

Interest-only loan Allows the monthly payment to be equal to only the interest charged for that particular month; the principal balance does not change.

Interest rate Percentage paid for the use of money, usually expressed as an annual percentage.

Liquidity Ease of converting real estate assets to cash.

Metropolitan statistical area (MSA) One or more counties that have a population of at least 50,000 residents.

Migration Refers to moves that cross state, division, or regional jurisdictional boundaries.

Miss-a-payment mortgage Borrowers are allowed to skip up to 2 mortgage payments a year, and up to 10 payments over the life of the loan without raising a credit concern.

Mixed-use communities Includes residential, retail, and commercial properties in a single development; it implies neighborhoods and towns with walkable streets that provide easy access to services and amenities such as schools, libraries, parks, and shops.

Mortgage A legal document that pledges a property to the lender as security for payment of a debt.

Mortgage interest deduction (MID) Tax break for people who pay mortgage interest on their homes.

Net migration The difference between immigration and out-migration in a given area during a specific period of time.

Option ARM A loan product that allows the borrower to pay less than the interest due; type of loan favored by investors.

Out-migration Migration out of an area for a certain period of time.

Piggyback loan A loan where a second mortgage is "piggybacked" onto the first mortgage; typically used when a buyer for a piece of real estate is unable to provide a large down payment or any down payment.

Price/earnings ratio (P/E) A ratio that is calculated by dividing the current share price of stock by the most recent figure for the earnings per share; the higher the figure, the more confident the investors.

Property tax Tax against the owner of some real estate.

Real property Legal name for the home, land, permanent structures, and all other rights included as the property for sale.

Rent-to-buy option Agreement between the owner of a property and the potential buyer whereby the rent or portion of the rent is applied to a down payment on the property at a certain date.

Rolling boom Speculative fever that moves from one real estate area to another—nationally or regionally.

Sale-in-lieu of foreclosure Also referred to as deed-in-lieu of foreclosure—situation where a property owner gives the deed to the lender without the lender having to go through the foreclosure process.

Sandwich generation A term often used to describe baby boomers since they are the generation that is often raising children while also taking responsibility for their aging parents.

Second-home buyer One who purchases a second residential property either for personal use (vacation or retirement) or for investment purposes.

Secondary market The purchase of existing mortgages by other lenders.

Sellers' market Situation where there are more buyers than homes for sale.

Starter home Beginning home that is less than what the buyer would prefer; typically used to build credit and experience in home ownership.

Urban renewal The rehabilitation of older, abandoned, or distressed city center areas; accomplished by tearing down older properties and building new commercial venues.

Valuation Estimated price or worth through appraisal.

Valuation Index Index that tracks home price appreciation patterns over decades to evaluate deviations from the historical norms.

LOCATING AND UNDERSTANDING ECONOMIC DATA

With the advent of the Internet, getting one's hands on current and meaningful economic numbers is easier than ever. But just like trying to compare mattresses among retailers, you will never really get all the information in one place. That said, it is challenging to know whether you are really comparing "firm" with "extra firm" and "pillow top" numbers.

The only way to overcome this is to make certain you understand the definitions that are being used. Government and economic statistics can be quite intimidating to the layperson unless they are decoded. For example, averages are not the same as medians. Averages are the total divided by the number of entries, whereas a median is the halfway point, where half is less and the other half is more than the median figure.

A typically confusing report is one that was issued in February 2006, the Federal Reserve's triennial Survey of Consumer Finances, where it was found that between 2001 and 2004, Americans earned less money and had more debt, yet net worth grew.

The median family income (half made more, half made less) rose only 1.6 percent to $43,200 in 2004, compared with 2001. Through 2003, the nation lost 2.7 million jobs and was coping with terrorist attacks, corporate scandals, and a recession. Average family incomes, after adjusting for inflation, fell from $72,346 in 2001 to $70,700 in 2004.

Meanwhile, American debt, as a percentage of total assets, rose to 15 percent in 2004, up from 12.1 percent in 2001. Mortgages were by far the biggest share of total debt at 75.2 percent in 2004, unchanged from the 2001 level.

So if incomes fell (to their lowest since 1992) and debt is higher, how could net worth rise by 6.3 percent? Net worth is the difference between assets and debt liabilities; and between 2001 and 2004, it was houses—not stocks—that buoyed Americans' wealth. The share of assets made up by home ownership rose to 50.3 percent in 2004, compared with 46.9 percent in 2001, while the share of financial assets because of stock investments dropped to 17.6 percent in 2004 down from 21.7 percent in 2001.

Now, after reading all that, would you conclude that families are in good or precarious shape? If you drew a conclusion, you'd be wrong because you don't yet have enough information. Families are in bad shape because the distribution of wealth isn't even across all incomes.

The wealthy got wealthier and the poor got poorer. The net worth of the top 10 percent of households rose by 6.1 percent to an average of $3.11 million, while the bottom 10 percent who were even-steven in 2001, now owed $1,400 more than their total assets in 2004.

The point is that no matter how much you know, there's always a data point that changes the interpretation.

Gathering economic information is expensive and time-consuming. Many sources may have fresh data, but it is not easily accessible, as they do not update their Web sites frequently. To be sure you are getting the latest information from an economic source, double-check the site's FAQs and online reports against press releases in its "newsroom." If fresher data is available, it will be there. If the site is not updated, notify the public relations contact.

Web Sites for Gathering Information

BEA.gov (Bureau of Economic Analysis) is an agency operated by the U.S. Department of Commerce. It collects economic data and makes reports about international transactions, balance of trade, international investment, gross domestic product (GDP), personal income, corporate profits, gross state product, state and personal income, and industry reports, including gross domestic product by industry.

BLS.gov (Bureau of Labor Statistics) provides data related to productivity including employment, unemployment, occupational outlooks, payroll data, and a key economic indicator for housing: the Consumer Price Index (CPI). Also included are wages, consumer spending, import/export prices, injury and illness data, and much more. Information can be drilled down to regional, state, and local employment figures.

census.gov (U.S. Census Bureau) gives a running U.S. occupancy count on the home page of its Web site and covers all statistics with regard to housing. (While some of its information is woefully out of date, the Bureau is attempting to find statistical means to extrapolate useful information.) Data is derived from public opinion polls, surveys, and focus groups, as well as studies contributed by the members.

cepr.net (Center for Economic and Policy Research) is an independent and privately funded think tank of doctorate-level researchers. It features a special section on its Web site about the "housing bubble." Cofounder Dean Baker, Ph.D., and others compare housing pricing and rents with jobs and household wealth to some "bubble warning" conclusions.

ciab.com (Council of Insurance Agents and Brokers) "represents leading commercial insurance agencies and brokerage firms to protect business, industry, government, and the public at-large."

consumerfed.org (Consumer Federation of America [CFA]) gathers "facts, analyzes issues, and disseminates information to the public, policy makers, and the rest of the consumer movement."

enterprisecommunity.org (Enterprise Community Partners) provides "investment capital and development services for affordable housing and community revitalization efforts," while "working in partnership with housing developers and corporate investors to invest equity in projects that qualify for low-income housing tax credits (LIHTC), a federal program enacted in 1986 that provides tax incentives for the private investment in decent, affordable rental housing."

Fanniemae.com (Fannie Mae) was established and chartered by the federal government as a privately owned entity with special legal status as a government-sponsored enterprise (GSE). Fannie Mae is a private, shareholder-owned company that is actively traded in the stock market. It works by insuring mortgages so loans will get made and buying back the mortgages and packaging them into securities to sell to Wall Street investors. Fannie Mae operates under congressional charter to increase home ownership for low-income to middle-income Americans. Fannie Mae's chief economist, David Berson, provides a monthly outlook.

Freddiemac.com (Freddie Mac) operates the same way as Fannie Mae; only to diversify risk, Freddie Mac guarantees different loans than Fannie Mae and packages them into different securities to sell to Wall Street. Freddie Mac's "Fact Book" is especially interesting for economic snapshots related to the mortgage industry, such as home buyer initiatives, credit information, predatory lending opposition, and delinquency rates. Freddie Mac's chief economist, Frank Nothaft, provides a monthly outlook.

habitat.org (Habitat for Humanity International) is a nonprofit, Christian housing ministry that seeks to "eliminate poverty and homelessness" and builds homes for people all over the world.

homeownershipalliance.com (Homeownership Alliance) is a coalition of many organizations "dedicated to preserving, protecting, and promoting expanded home ownership opportunities for all Americans."

icba.org (Independent Community Bankers of America) is an organization of "community banks of all sizes and charter types dedicated exclusively to protecting the interests of the community banking industry."

iiaa.org (Independent Insurance Agents and Brokers of America) is an organization whose members are "independent insurance agents and insurance brokers" that "represent more than one insurance company, so they can offer clients a wider choice of auto, home, business, life, and health coverage as well as retirement and employee-benefit products."

jchs.harvard.edu (The Joint Center for Housing Studies) is Harvard University's center for information and research on housing in the United States. Run by senior faculty with backgrounds in economics, demographics, and finance, the center analyzes relationships between housing markets and the current economic, demographic, and social trends. It provides leaders in government, business, and the nonprofit sector with knowledge to develop specific policies and strategies. Excellent reading is the center's "State of the Nation's Housing," which is released annually.

lisc.org (Local Initiatives Support Corporation) helps "resident-led, community-based development organizations transform distressed communities and neighborhoods into healthy ones—good places to live, do business, work, and raise families" by "providing capital, technical expertise, training, and information, LISC supports the development of local leadership and the creation of affordable housing, commercial, industrial, and community facilities, businesses, and jobs. We help neighbors build communities."

MBAA.org (The Mortgage Bankers Association [MBA]) produces documents and analysis of details such as its housing and mortgage markets report, state and local news, and mortgage and economic forecasts. There is a broad set of available data on mortgage markets and real estate markets for both the residential and commercial real estate and real estate finance industries. The data is collected from proprietary MBA surveys and public data sources for the use of people interested in the markets.

nafcunet.org (National Association of Federal Credit Unions) represents the interests of federal credit unions before the federal government and the public with "information, education, and assistance to meet the challenges that cooperative financial institutions face in today's economic environment."

NAHB.org (The National Association of Home Builders [NAHB]) provides excellent information about new home builders and remodelers, such as what to expect when you hire a builder, how to build a home, home maintenance tips, all about custom homes, all about building materials, and other news and information. The organization provides information to the popular press to benefit its members, consumers, and local communities. NAHB operates a blog at nahbblog.blogs.com.

nahrep.org (National Association of Hispanic Real Estate Professionals) promotes training for Hispanic real estate professionals to empower Hispanic home buying/selling consumers.

namb.org (National Association of Mortgage Brokers [NAMB]) supports small business–oriented mortgage brokers to manage their businesses and promote home ownership.

nareb.com (National Association of Real Estate Brokers [NAREB]) serves minority real estate professionals to offer "economic improvement for both our members and the minority community we serve."

nationalbankers.org (National Bankers Association) is a trade association for minority- and women-owned banks (MWOBs). These MWOBs "serve distressed communities" by "providing employment opportunities, entrepreneurial capital, and economic revitalization in neighborhoods which often have little or no access to alternative financial services."

nclr.org (National Council of La Raza) is a Latino civil rights organization that works to improve opportunities for Latinos.

NHC.org (The National Housing Conference) is a nonprofit consumer advocacy group for housing and public policy. The Center for Housing Policy is the NHC's research affiliate, but it does not have a separate Web site. The NHC and Center for Housing Policy delve into such research topics as housing for working families, families with children, affordability, and community issues. Such studies may be funded by Freddie Mac or other supporters and patrons.

nul.org (National Urban League) empowers "African Americans to enter the economic and social mainstream."

Realtor.org (The National Association of REALTORS® [NAR]) is a trade organization representing over 1.2 million members. In addition to the Web site, the NAR is also a terrific source of ongoing research, such as its Insights product, a monthly newsletter full of text, tidbits, and tantalizing forecasts. The monthly list of leading economic indicators at Realtor.org is found under the Research button. The Web address www.realtor.org/research.nsf/pages/EcoIndicator?OpenDocument will take you directly to the most current information on the following:

- *Existing home sales (EHS)*—defined as approximately 85 percent of housing sales
- *Pending sales*—those existing home sales that are under contract, but have yet to close escrow
- *New-home sales*—new-home transactions that are under contract and not closed (involve properties purchased directly from builders)
- *Housing starts*—homes that have begun construction (digging)
- *Mortgage interest rates*—the loan rates and terms that borrowers can lock in that day, at that moment
- *Mortgage applications*—the number of applications (not approvals) for loans

wfca.org (World Floor Covering Association [WFCA]) is a nonprofit educational organization for consumers to learn more about flooring options.

Whitehouse.gov is the online White House Briefing Room that offers snapshots of crucial economic data—particularly jobs, households, money, and output. The data comes primarily from the Bureau of Labor Statistics, U.S. Census Bureau, Federal Reserve Board, and the Bureau of Economic Analysis (an agency of the U.S. Department of Commerce).

INDEX

About the Author

Blanche Evans is the editor of *Realty Times* (www.realtytimes.com), a contributor to *Realty Times* TV, and a sought-after speaker, pundit, and source for the real estate industry and the national media.

Blanche and *Realty Times* are the go-to Internet source for consumer and industry real estate news and advice. Independently owned and operated, *Realty Times* is not only a leading content provider but also the sponsor of *Realty Times* TV, a daily show that provides home buying and selling news and advice to consumers while showcasing Realtor listings from around the country.

A former sales trainer, Blanche began her writing career as a freelance business and PR writer in 1993 and soon started her own business, Newbury Communications. Assignments kept coming for real estate–related articles, and Blanche realized she had found her calling. In 1997, she joined *Realty Times* as its sole correspondent and editor. Since then, *Realty Times* has grown into the largest real estate news service on the Internet with staff in California; Washington, D.C.; Nevada; and Texas.

Since joining *Realty Times,* Blanche has been recognized by the editors of *REALTOR®* magazine as one of the "25 Most Influential People in Real Estate" and one of the few women recognized at the "Notable" level or above more than once. She was recognized by Delahaye-Bacon in 2005 as the top reporter covering the National Association of REALTORS®.

With Blanche's influence, *Realty Times* has garnered several awards, including recognition by *Money Magazine*'s "Best of the Web: Buying and Selling," June 2003, and "Best Real Estate News," Yahoo! Internet Life, March 2002.

Blanche has bought, improved, and sold houses in every kind of buyers' and sellers' markets in Dallas, Texas. She speaks firsthand about how a home is not only a place to live and raise a family, but that home owning can be a great hedge against financial hard times and a way to build personal wealth.

Today, Blanche is finding new direction as an author of numerous books, magazine articles, and white papers about the real estate industry and is a well received speaker at industry events. She is frequently interviewed about consumer real estate issues, including appearances on CNN, and is widely regarded as one of the most knowledgeable people in the real estate industry.

Blanche has also been tapped to write the official home buying and selling guides for The National Association of REALTORS®, in the fall of 2006. Her next project will be a work of fiction noir called *Urban Renewal*.